Basic ESL
Workbook

The companion book to Basic ESL *Online*:
www.basicesl.com

LEVEL 1

C. Sesma, M. A.
ESL and Spanish Teacher

Bilingual Dictionaries, Inc.

Basic ESL® Workbook: Level 1
English as a Second Language

Publisher:
Bilingual Dictionaries, Inc.
P.O.Box 1154
Murrieta, CA 92564
Website: www.bilingualdictionaries.com
Email: support@bilingualdictionaries.com

Content by C. Sesma, M.A.
English and Spanish Teacher

Design by John Garcia

ISBN13: 978-0-933146-14-3
ISBN: 0-933146-14-0

The **Basic ESL® Workbooks** are the companion books to **Basic ESL® Online.**
Basic ESL Online provides:
> Online English Learning
> Audio Pronunciation of English
> Native Language Support

For **information** and **registration** to Basic ESL® Online please visit the the Basic ESL® website:
Website: www.BasicESL.com
Email: info@basicesl.com

Printed in India

Prologue

The **Basic ESL Workbook** is the companion book to **Basic ESL Online (www.basicesl.com)**. Except for the English pronunciations and native language translations that are provided online, this book follows the online course content with some adjustments required by the book format. Since written grammatical exercises cannot be provided online, this book has added an extra section at the end of each lesson. The written exercises section provides the ability to test the student's progress and knowledge of the English language structure. In order for the student to get the best of Basic ESL, it is very important to be familiar with the goals and learning methods of the online lessons found at www.basicesl.com.

The **main goal** of Basic ESL Online is to develop the oral skills of communication rather than trying to memorize grammatical rules. The first oral skill of communication is **to be able to understand the spoken English**. This is accomplished by continuous listening to the oral exercises, stories, dialogs and conversations. The second and most important oral skill of communication is **to be able to ask and answer questions.**

To accomplish these goals, Basic ESL offers simple and effective learning methods that will help the student succeed in learning English as a Second Language:

1. The gradual, step by step approach of learning the English language. Each lesson is built on the knowledge of the previous lessons, in addition to the new content for that lesson.

2. The Lesson Sections (A-H): the vocabulary study, the sentence structure, the listening exercises, the conversation exercises and the presentation of common phrases used by native English speakers.

3. The English Pronunciation. At Basic ESL Online, the students are in control of the English pronunciation by allowing them to listen and repeat all the words and sentences as many times as needed.

4. The Translations. The translation of the English vocabulary and sentence structures into the native language of the student will speed up the process of learning English. The translations are also a great tool for self-study at home or at the local library.

5. The Explanation of Grammatical Concepts. Students who want to learn the mechanics of the language will find grammar concepts explained in their native language. By clicking on the **information button** [i] at Basic ESL Online, students can view the translated grammar concepts that go along with the lesson.

The Basic ESL Workbook works together with Basic ESL Online (www.basicesl.com) to give English language learners a simple and effective way to learn English as a second language. Basic ESL Online provides the audio English pronunciation for the different lesson sections as well as the written native language translations. We strongly recommend all Basic ESL students to register for Basic ESL Online at www.basicesl.com.

Recommendation to the Student

In order to obtain the best results from the use of this Basic ESL Workbook, we recommend the student becomes a member of **Basic ESL Online** at:

www.basicesl.com

Here the student will find the audio English pronunciations, the native language translation support of the vocabulary and the sentence structures, plus the grammar explanations in the language of the student.

Contents

Chapter 1
The Family

Lesson 1:   Family Members
Lesson 2:   Their Description
Lesson 3:   Their Age

What to do in each section of every lesson...

A - Vocabulary Study

Section A includes the vocabulary that will be used throughout the lesson. Learning new vocabulary is basic to learning a new language.

Read the vocabulary several times.
If you are on Basic ESL Online:
Listen to the **English audio pronunciation**.
View the **native language translations** of the vocabulary.

Listen and read the vocabulary until you can understand the vocabulary without looking at the words.

B - Sentence Structure

Section B teaches students basic English sentences using the vocabulary in section A.

Read and **study** the sentences.
If you are on Basic ESL Online:
Listen to the **English audio pronunciation**.
View the **native language translations** of the sentences.
View the **grammar concepts** by clicking on the **information button** .

Repeat the sentences as many times as needed. Continue to the next section once you can **understand** the sentences without looking at them.

C - Listening Exercises

Read the story or dialog several times.
If you are on Basic ESL Online, **listen** to the story or dialog while reading it several times.

Once you are familiar with the story or dialog, try to see if you can **understand** it by only listening without reading.

D - Conversation Exercises

Read the conversation dialogs several times.
If you are on Basic ESL Online, **listen** to the dialogs until you can understand them without looking at them.

Finally, try to **speak** the conversation dialogs by only looking at the pictures and key words.

E - Common Phrases

Many of the **common phrases** that are presented in this section are frequently used by the native English speakers in their everyday life.

Read the common phrases several times.
If you are on Basic ESL Online, **listen** to the common phrases while reading. **Listen** as many times as needed until you can understand the common phrases without looking at the sentences.

H - Written Exercises

The written exercises provide an opportunity to test what you learned in the lesson. You can never be sure of knowing something unless you can put it in writing.

You can check your answers by going to the **Answer Key Section** in the back of the workbook.

For information regarding **Basic ESL Online,** please visit **www.basicesl.com**.
Audio Pronunciaton of English & Native Language Translations.

Lesson #1

Family Members

Index

Audio & Translations

 English Audio available online for sections A-E.

 Translations in various Languages available online for Sections A, B, and E.

www.BasicESL.com

1. father

2. mother

3. uncle

4. aunt

5. brother

6. sister

7. son

8. daughter

9. nephew

10. niece

11. husband

12. wife

13. grandmother

14. grandfather

15. brother-in-law

16. sister-in-law

17. relative

18. cousin

19. granddaughter

20. grandson

Other Vocabulary

1.	n	friend	**11.**	adj	his
2.	n	name	**12.**	adj	your
3.	n	Spain	**13.**	adj	this
4.	n	France	**14.**	v	love
5.	adj	Mexican	**15.**	v	repeat
6.	adj	previous	**16.**	v	listen
7.	adj	next	**17.**	adv	here
8.	adj	big	**18.**	adv	also
9.	adj	last	**19.**	pre	from
10.	adj	her	**20.**	pre	of

For the audio pronunciations and written translations of **Sections A and B,** please go to:

www.basicesl.com

B1. Nouns: Singular (S) and Plural (P)

S	the mother
P	the mothers
S	the relative
P	the relatives
S	the niece
P	the nieces
S	the brother
P	the brothers

B1 - B2

Nouns are words used to name people, things or places.

In English, plural nouns are formed by adding an "**-s**" to the singular form of the noun.

There are several **exceptions** that will be learned in lesson 8.

B2. Nouns: Singular (S) and Plural (P)

S	the father
P	the fathers
S	the sister
P	the sisters
S	the aunt
P	the aunts
S	the cousin
P	the cousins

B3 - B4

An **article** *is an adjective that goes in front of a noun to indicate if it refers to a specific noun or not. Articles have no plural forms in English. There are two types of articles:*

The **definite article "the"** *is used with specific or particular nouns.*

The **indefinite article "a"** *or* **"an"** *is used with a singular noun that does not refer to a specific noun.* **"An"** *is used in front of a noun that begins with a vowel.* **"A"** *is used if the noun begins with a consonant.*

B3. Articles: Definite (D) and Indefinite (I)

D	**the** lesson
I	**a** lesson
D	**the** uncle
I	**an** uncle
D	**the** mother
I	**a** mother
D	**the** aunt
I	**an** aunt

B4. Articles: Definite (D) and Indefinite (I)

D	**the** exercise
I	**an** exercise
D	**the** chapter
I	**a** chapter
D	**the** husband
I	**a** husband
D	**the** wife
I	**a** wife

B5. Subject Pronouns

	I
	you
Singular	he
	she
	it
	we
Plural	you
	they

B6. Verb "to be": Present Tense

	I	**am**	Susan.
	You	**are**	Tony.
Singular	He	**is**	Henry.
	She	**is**	Mary
	It	**is**	big.
	We	**are**	cousins.
Plural	You	**are**	brothers.
	They	**are**	sisters.

B3 - B4 (continued)

B5

Pronouns are words that re-place nouns. The *subject pronouns* are those that perform the action of the verb.

B6

The word **verb** indicates an action. The verb **"to be"** indicates a quality or existence.

The **tense** of the verb indicates when the action of the verb takes place. There are three tenses: present, past and future.

The **present tense** indicates actions that are happening at the time of speaking, or express a quality of the subject also present at the time of speaking.

C1. Read and Listen to the story.

My name is Juan. I am Mexican. My family is from Mexico. My sister is Mexican also. Mary and Jose are my aunt and uncle. They are from Spain.

My nephews and my niece are here. They are Mexican. My grandmother and my grandfather are here also.

Mexico and Spain

D1. sister / Helen Rice

This is my sister.

What is her name?
Her name is Helen.

What is her last name?
Her last name is Rice.

D2. uncle / Tony Gomez

This is my uncle.

What is his name?
His name is Tony.

What is his last name?
His last name is Gomez.

D3. cousin / Mike Brown

This is my cousin.

What is his name?
His name is Mike.

What is his last name?
His last name is Brown.

D4. niece / Susan Mendes

This is my niece.

What is her name?
Her name is Susan.

What is her last name?
Her last name is Mendes.

Greetings

1. Good morning.
2. Good afternoon.
3. Good evening.
4. Good night.
5. Happy New Year!
6. Merry Christmas!
7. Happy Birthday!
8. Happy Easter!
9. Congratulations!

For the English audio pronunciations and written native language translations of **section E,** please go to:

www.basicesl.com

Merry Christmas

Happy Birthday

End of the **oral exercises** for lesson 1.
You can find additional exercises in sections D, F & G at Basic ESL Online.

Please continue with the **written exercises** for this lesson in **section H.**

Lesson

1

H1. Change to the plural.

1.	the sister	*the sisters*
2.	the aunt	_____
3.	the husband	_____
4.	the nephew	_____
5.	the sentence	_____
6.	the niece	_____
7.	the brother	_____
8.	the lesson	_____
9.	the exercise	_____
10.	the mother	_____
11.	the article	_____
12.	the cousin	_____
13.	the father	_____
14.	the daughter	_____
15.	the relative	_____

H2. Article a or an.

1.	*a*	sister
2.	_____	aunt
3.	_____	husband
4.	_____	nephew
5.	_____	sentence
6.	_____	niece
7.	_____	brother
8.	_____	lesson
9.	_____	exercise
10.	_____	mother
11.	_____	article
12.	_____	cousin
13.	_____	father
14.	_____	daughter
15.	_____	relative

H3. Complete with the verb "to be".

1. Mary **is** my sister.
2. You _____ my brother.
3. She _____ my mother.
4. I _____ your niece.
5. He _____ Tony
6. They _____ friends.
7. My name _____ Henry.
8. We _____ here.
9. My daughter _____ here.
10. Your son _____ in Mexico.
11. He _____ Mexican.
12. His name _____ Henry.
13. I _____ Susan.
14. My family _____ from Spain.
15. You _____ from Spain also.
16. We _____ big.

Practice Writing

H4. Change to the plural.

1. she _____
2. I _____
3. you _____
4. he _____
5. it _____

Lesson #2

Their Description

Audio & Translations

 English Audio available online for sections A-E.

 Translations in various Languages available online for Sections A, B, and E.

www.BasicESL.com

1. tall

2. short

3. fat

4. thin

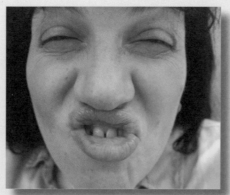

5. ugly

6. beautiful

7. rich

8. poor

9. happy

10. sad

11. young

12. old

13. married

14. single

15. handsome

16. smart

17. funny

18. serious

19. bald

20. shy

21. pretty

Other Vocabulary

1.	n	description	10.	adj	strong
2.	n	conversation	11.	adj	weak
3.	n	sentence	12.	adj	brave
4.	n	thing	13.	adj	divorced
5.	n	question	14.	adj	polite
6.	n	answer	15.	v	be
7.	n	nationality	16.	v	change
8.	adj	bad	17.	v	replace
9.	adj	long	18.	adv	very

For the audio pronunciations and written translations of **Sections A and B,** please go to:

www.basicesl.com

B1. Describing People

The son is **tall**.
The daughter is **short**.

The uncle is **fat**.
The aunt is **thin**.

The brothers are **good**.
The sister is **smart**.

The nephews are **sad**.
The nieces are **happy**.

B1

Adjectives are words used to describe nouns.

B2. Subject Nouns (N) and Pronouns (P)

N	**The nieces** are bad.
P	**They** are bad.
N	**The father** is good.
P	**He** is good.
N	**The sister** is beautiful.
P	**She** is beautiful.
N	**Joe** is fat.
P	**He** is fat.

B2 - B3

Pronouns are words used in place of nouns.

The **subject** is the noun or pronoun that performs the action of the verb. The subject always goes in front of the verb.

The **subject pronoun** is a noun that replaces a subject noun.

B3. Subject Nouns (N) and Pronouns (P)

N	**The lesson** is short.
P	**It** is short.
N	**The lessons** are long.
P	**They** are long.
N	**Helen** and **I** are smart.
P	**We** are smart.
N	**Tom** and **Mary** are young.
P	**They** are young.

B4. Verb "to be": Negative Sentences (NS)

	I **am** thin.
NS	I **am not** fat.
	You **are** pretty.
NS	You **are not** ugly.
	He **is** strong.
NS	He **is not** weak.
	She **is** happy.
NS	She **is not** sad.

B4 - B5

Negative sentences with the verb "to be" are formed with the word "not" after the verb.

B5. Verb "to be": Negative Sentences (NS)

	We **are** good.
NS	We **are not** bad.
	They **are** married.
NS	They **are not** single.
	John **is** tall.
NS	He **is not** short.
	Mary **is** poor.
NS	She **is not** rich.

B6. Asking for descriptions.

What is Mary **like**?
She is tall.
What are you **like**?
I am short.
What is Peter **like**?
He is handsome.
What is Margaret **like**?
She is beautiful.

B6

When we want to obtain information about the description of a person or thing, we use the interrogative words "What ... like?"

C1. Read and Listen to the Story.

Greg is my brother. He is smart and strong. He is not weak. He is from Mexico. His nationality is Mexican. Susan is my sister. She is small and thin. She is not big. My two nieces are Sara and Mary. Sara is short and beautiful. Sara is not tall.

Fred is big and fat. He is not small. Tom is handsome. He is not ugly. I am young. I am not old. My uncle Tony is rich. He is not poor. My aunt is not rich. She is poor. My grandmother is happy. She is not sad.

The school is big. It is not small. The schools in America are pretty. They are not ugly.

C2. Read and Listen to the dialog.

What is your son like?
    He is young.

What is your sister like?
    She is beautiful.

What are your cousins like?
    They are okay.

What is your niece like?
    She's pretty and happy.

What are your parents like?
    They are tall and thin.

What is your aunt like?
    She is rich.

What is your uncle like?
    He is poor.

What is your grandmother like?
    She is old.

D1. uncle Bob / handsome

This is my uncle.

What is his name?
His name is Bob.

What is he like?
He is handsome.

D2. sister Lisa / beautiful

This is my sister?

What is her name?
Her name is Lisa.

What is she like?
She is beautiful.

D3. grandfather Henry / old

This is my grandfather.

What is his name?
His name is Henry.

What is he like?
He is old.

D4. aunt Carol / short

This is my aunt.

What is her name?
He name is Carol.

What is she like?
She is short.

Describing People

1. **What is Mary like?**
2. **She is pretty.**
3. **She is sweet.**
4. **She is honest.**
5. **She is shy.**
6. **She is proud.**
7. **She is generous.**
8. **She is silly.**
9. **She is naive.**
10. **She is friendly.**

For the English audio pronunciations and written native language translations of **section E,** please go to:

www.basicesl.com

She is friendly.

She is pretty.

End of the **oral exercises** for lesson 2.

You can find additional exercises in sections D, F & G at Basic ESL Online.

Please continue with the **written exercises** for this lesson in **section H.**

Lesson

2

H1. Write the opposite adjectives.

1.	rich	*poor*	7.	thin	
2.	tall	_____	8.	ugly	_____
3.	handsome	_____	9.	old	_____
4.	big	_____	10.	small	_____
5.	married	_____	11.	happy	_____
6.	pretty	_____	12.	poor	_____

H2. Write the masculine noun.

1.	wife	*husband*	6.	grandmother	_____
2.	aunt	_____	7.	daughter	_____
3.	niece	_____	8.	sister-in-law	_____
4.	mother	_____	9.	cousin	_____
5.	sister	_____	10.	relative	_____

H3. **Replace the** subject nouns **with subject** pronouns.

1.	The **lessons** are short.	*They are short.*
2.	**Mary** is pretty.	
3.	The **lesson** is long.	
4.	**John** is tall.	
5.	My **son** is single.	
6.	Our **brothers** are good.	
7.	His **niece** is strong.	
8.	The **boy** is young.	
9.	**Sara** is thin.	
10.	**Sara** and **Ann** are tall.	
11.	**Tom** and **I** are smart.	
12.	The **school** is not big.	
13.	**Mike** and **you** are students.	
14.	Your **family** is rich.	
15.	**Pat** and **Susan** are pretty.	
16.	My **cousin** is not ugly.	
17.	The **lesson** is long.	
18.	**Greg** and **Mary** are bad.	
19.	**Fred** is handsome.	
20.	**Henry** and **you** are rich.	
21.	**Henry** and **I** are brothers.	
22.	Her **grandfather** is old.	
23.	The **sentence** is short.	
24.	The **sentences** are long.	
25.	Your **daughter** is polite.	

H4. Make the sentence negative. Use the opposite adjective.

1. Mary is rich.   *Mary is **not** poor.*
2. You are tall.   _____
3. She is pretty.   _____
4. I am single.   _____
5. He is happy.   _____
6. They are thin.   _____
7. We are handsome.   _____

H5. Make correct sentences with the correct form of the verb.

1. tall-Pat-be-Steven-and   *Pat and Steven are tall.*
2. nephew-be-the-small   _____
3. cousin-his-not-be-you   _____
4. Mary-like-be-what ?   _____
5. happy-I-and-tall-be   _____
6. brother-be-the-ugly-not   _____
7. he-not-be-brother-my   _____

H6. Complete with the verb "to be".

#	Subject		Adjective	Answer
1.	The family	*is*	good.	is
2.	It	_____	bad.	is
3.	Sara	_____	young.	is not
4.	She	_____	old.	is not
5.	My brothers	_____	married.	are not
6.	They	_____	single.	are

H7. Follow the example.

1.   Tom

   thin

   What is Tom like?

   He is thin.

   He is not fat.

2.   grandfather

   old

   _____

   _____

   _____

3.   Lisa - Carol

   married

   _____

   _____

   _____

4.   you

   tall

   _____

   _____

   _____

5.   sisters

   beautiful

   _____

   _____

   _____

Lesson #3

Their Age

Index

Audio & Translations

 English Audio available online for sections A-E.

 Translations in various Languages available online for Sections A, B, and E.

www.BasicESL.com

1. one

2. two

3. three

4. four

5. five

6. six

7. seven

8. eight

9. nine

10	**11**	**12**
10. ten	**11.** eleven	**12.** twelve
13	**14**	**15**
13. thirteen	**14.** fourteen	**15.** fifteen
16	**17**	**18**
16. sixteen	**17.** seventeen	**18.** eighteen

19	**20**	**21**
19. nineteen	20. twenty	21. twenty-one

Other Vocabulary

1.	n	chapter	10.	adj	same
2.	n	verb	11.	adj	different
3.	n	article	12.	adj	coward
4.	n	phone	13.	adj	funny
5.	n	number	14.	adj	serious
6.	n	England	15.	adj	kind
7.	n	France	16.	adj	mean
8.	n	story	17.	adj	intelligent
9.	n	Italy	18.	adv	especially

For the audio pronunciations and written translations of **Sections A and B**, please go to:

www.basicesl.com

B1. Age: Numbers 1-20

12	Tony is **twelve** years old.
11	He is not **eleven** years old.
13	Sara is **thirteen** years old.
14	She is not **fourteen** years old.
1	Ann is **one** year old.
3	She is not **three** years old.
16	Greg and Mike are **sixteen** years old.
15	They are not **fifteen** years old.

B2. Age: Numbers 1-20

5	Ann is **five** years old.
6	She is not **six** years old.
8	I am **eight** years old.
7	I am not **seven** years old.
10	Mary and I are **ten** years old.
9	We are not **nine** years old.
4	You and Karen are **four** years old.
2	You are not **two** years old.

B1- B2

Adjectives are words that describe and accompany nouns. **Numbers** *belong to the family of adjectives. They indicate the number of people or things.*

B3. Question words: "how old"

How old are you?
I am **twelve** years old.

How old is my uncle?
He is **twenty-one** years old.

How old is Cynthia?
She is **nine** years old.

How old are my cousins?
They are **thirteen** years old.

B3

When we want to obtain information about the age of someone or something, we use the question words **"how old."**

B4. Possessive Adjectives

Singular	my
	your
	his
	her
	its
Plural	our
	your
	their

B4

Adjectives are words used to describe nouns.

Possessive adjectives are those that indicate possession.

B5. Verb "to love": Present Tense

Singular	I	love.
	You	love.
	He	loves.
	She	loves.
Plural	We	love.
	You	love.
	They	love.

B5

A *verb* indicates an action.

The *tense* indicates when the action of the verb takes place. There are three tenses: present, past and future. The *present tense* indicates actions that are happening at the time of speaking.

The *form* of the verb in the present tense is the same for all subjects, except the 3rd Person singular: *he, she, it* or a *noun singular*. In this case we add an "*-s*" to the verb.

B6. Possessive Adjectives (PA) and Subject Pronouns (SP)

SP	Verb	PA	
I	love	my	son.
You	love	**your**	daughter.
He	loves	**his**	sister.
She	loves	**her**	brother.
We	love	**our**	father
You	love	**your**	parents.
They	love	**their**	nephew.

B6

Possessive adjectives indicate to whom something belongs. This exercise shows the relation between the subject pronoun and the corresponding possessive adjective when the thing or person possessed belongs to the subject.

C1. Read and Listen to the Story.

Tom and **Greg** are my friends. **They** are young. **Their** nationality is French. **They** come from France. **They** are tall and smart. **Their** uncles live in France. Tom and Greg love **their** family and **their** family love them.

Tom and Greg live with **their** parents and sisters. **Their** parents are very good, especially **their** mother.

Other relatives of Tom and Greg are **their** cousin Alice, **their** niece Susan and **their** aunt Mary. Alice is short and beautiful. Susan is pretty and nice. **Their** aunt is rich and happy.

C2. Read and Listen to the Story.

Tom is my friend. **He** is young. **His** nationality is French. **He** comes from France. **He** is tall and smart. **His** uncles live in France. **Tom** loves **his** family and **his** family loves Tom.

Tom lives with **his** parents and sisters. **His** parents are very nice, especially **his** mother.

Other relatives of Tom are **his** cousin Alice, **his** niece Susan and **his** aunt Mary. Alice is short and beautiful. Susan is very pretty and nice. **His** aunt is rich and happy.

D1. uncle / 26 / happy

How old is your uncle?
He is 26 years old.

What is your uncle like?
He is happy.

What is your aunt like?
She is not happy. She is sad.

D2. sisters / 12 / thin

How old are your sisters?
They are 12 years old.

What are your sisters like?
They are thin.

What are your brothers like?
They are not thin. They are fat.

D3. mother / 28 / young

How old is your mother?
She is 28 years old.

What is your mother like?
She is young.

What is your father like?
He is not young. He is old.

D4. nephew / 11 / funny

How old is your nephew?
He is 11 years old.

What is your nephew like?
He is funny.

What is your niece like?
She is not funny. She is serious.

Describing People

1. **What is Tony like?**
2. **He is stubborn.**
3. **He is quiet.**
4. **He is trustworthy.**
5. **He is kind.**
6. **He is clever.**
7. **He is stingy.**
8. **He is nervous.**
9. **He is unfriendly.**
10. **He is lazy.**

For the English audio pronunciations and written native language translations of **section E,** please go to:

www.basicesl.com

He is trustworthy.

He is clever.

End of the **oral exercises** for lesson 3.

You can find additional exercises in sections D, F & G at Basic ESL Online.

Please continue with the **written exercises** for this lesson in **section H.**

Training

Lesson

3

H1. Complete with the verb "to love".

1. I	*love*	Lucy.
2. You	_____	the lesson.
3. He	_____	Mary.
4. She	_____	the school.
5. We	_____	Italy.
6. They	_____	Mexico.
7. Mary	_____	France.
8. Tony	_____	his daughter.
9. The boys	_____	England.
10. Sara	_____	Spain.
11. Sara and I	_____	England.
12. Sara and you	_____	Mexico.
13. Sara and Pat	_____	the story.
14. You and I	_____	the dialogs.
15. Jason	_____	his family.

H2. Opposites

1. rich	*poor*
2. small	_____
3. tall	_____
4. big	_____
5. single	_____
6. ugly	_____
7. fat	_____
8. beautiful	_____
9. daughter	_____
10. father	_____
11. brother	_____
12. usband	_____
13. cousin	_____
14. uncle	_____
15. old	_____

H3. Write the correct form of the verbs.

1.	listen	I	*listen* to my father.
2.	come	My sister	_____ from France.
3.	live	You	_____ in Spain.
4.	love	My sisters	_____ the school.
5.	start	Mary	_____ lesson one.
6.	come	Mary and I	_____ from Mexico
7.	love	We	_____ our family.
8.	live	Henry	_____ in France.
9.	live	The uncles	_____ in Spain.
10.	listen	She	_____ to her teacher.
11.	live	Tony	_____ in France.
12.	love	He	_____ France.
13.	start	It	_____ here.
14.	come	Mary	_____ from Mexico.
15.	love	She	_____ Mexico.
16.	live	You	_____ in Spain.
17.	live	Your mother	_____ here.
18.	listen	My friend	_____ to Mary.
19.	repeat	My friends	_____ the lessons.
20.	memorize	Henry	_____ the lesson.
21.	ask	He	_____ the questions.
22.	love	Sara	_____ Spanish.
23.	come	I	_____ from France.

H4. Write the possessive adjective.

1. John loves   *his*   sister
2. The students love _____ school.
3. You love   _____ school.
4. Henry lives with _____ nephew.
5. The sister loves _____ family.
6. Tony loves   _____ sons.
7. They love   _____ daughter.
8. Mary and Lucy love _____ grandmother.
9. She loves   _____ father.
10. He lives with   _____ mother.
11. The boys live with _____ aunt.
12. The husband loves _____ wife.
13. The wife loves   _____ husband.
14. You live with   _____ relatives.
15. We live with   _____ sister.
16. They love   _____ granddaughter.
17. Mary and Lucy love _____ brother-in-law.
18. I listen to   _____ parents.
19. They listen to   _____ parents.
20. Tom and I live with _____ parents.
21. Sara loves   _____ parents.
22. You love   _____ grandmother.
23. You and Sara love _____ grandfather.
24. My sisters practice _____ exercises.

H5. Numbers

1. *one*
2. _____
3. _____
4. _____
5. _____
6. _____
7. _____
8. _____
9. _____
10. _____
11. _____
12. _____
13. _____
14. _____
15. _____
16. _____
17. _____
18. _____
19. _____
20. _____
21. _____
22. _____
23. _____
24. _____

H6. **Change** Ann **for** Tom.

Ann is my friend. She comes from France. Her uncles live in France. **Ann** loves her family and her family loves **Ann.**

Ann lives with her parents and two other sisters. The parents love their daughter **Ann** and she loves her parents also, especially her mother.

Other relatives of **Ann** are: her cousin Alice, her niece Susan and Ray her nephew.

Tom is my friend. _____

_____

_____

_____

_____

_____

_____

_____

_____

_____

_____

_____

_____

_____

_____

_____

_____

_____

_____

_____

End of the **Lesson 3**

Chapter 2
The School

Lesson 4:   People and Places
Lesson 5:   School Subjects
Lesson 6:   School Objects

What to do in each section of every lesson...

A - Vocabulary Study

Section A includes the vocabulary that will be used throughout the lesson. Learning new vocabulary is basic to learning a new language.

Read the vocabulary several times.
If you are on Basic ESL Online:
Listen to the **English audio pronunciation**.
View the **native language translations** of the vocabulary.

Listen and read the vocabulary until you can understand the vocabulary without looking at the words.

B - Sentence Structure

Section B teaches students basic English sentences using the vocabulary in section A.

Read and **study** the sentences.
If you are on Basic ESL Online:
Listen to the **English audio pronunciation**.
View the **native language translations** of the sentences.
View the **grammar concepts** by clicking on the **information button** .

Repeat the sentences as many times as needed. Continue to the next section once you can **understand** the sentences without looking at them.

C - Listening Exercises

Read the story or dialog several times.
If you are on Basic ESL Online, **listen** to the story or dialog while reading it several times.

Once you are familiar with the story or dialog, try to see if you can **understand** it by only listening without reading.

D - Conversation Exercises

Read the conversation dialogs several times.
If you are on Basic ESL Online, **listen** to the dialogs until you can understand them without looking at them.

Finally, try to **speak** the conversation dialogs by only looking at the pictures and key words.

E - Common Phrases

Many of the **common phrases** that are presented in this section are frequently used by the native English speakers in their everyday life.

Read the common phrases several times.
If you are on Basic ESL Online, **listen** to the common phrases while reading. **Listen** as many times as needed until you can understand the common phrases without looking at the sentences.

H - Written Exercises

The written exercises provide an opportunity to test what you learned in the lesson. You can never be sure of knowing something unless you can put it in writing.

You can check your answers by going to the **Answer Key Section** in the back of the workbook.

For information regarding **Basic ESL Online,** please visit **www.basicesl.com**.
Audio Pronunciaton of English & Native Language Translations.

Lesson #4

People and Places

Audio & Translations

English Audio available online for sections A-E.

Translations in various Languages available online for Sections A, B, and E.

www.BasicESL.com

1. principal

2. teacher

3. janitor

4. coach

5. student

6. secretary

7. librarian

8. nurse

9. patio

10. classroom

11. restroom

12. auditorium

13. playground

14. library

15. gymnasium

16. cafeteria

17. office

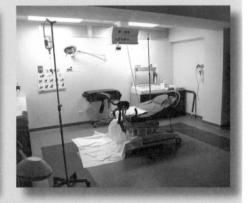

18. clinic

19. counselor

20. people

Other Vocabulary

1.	n	pupil	**10.**	v	sit
2.	n	end	**11.**	v	speak
3.	n	fault	**12.**	v	study
4.	n	boy	**13.**	v	draw
5.	n	girl	**14.**	v	erase
6.	adj	first	**15.**	v	teach
7.	adj	main	**16.**	adv	now
8.	v	begin	**17.**	adv	late
9.	v	say	**18.**	con	because

For the Audio pronunciations and written translations of **Sections A and B,** please go to:

www.basicesl.com

Looking for Bilingual Dictionaries?
You can find a large selection at:

www.bilingualdictionaries.com

B1. Verb "to be": Affirmative Contractions (AC)

	I am a teacher.
AC	I'm a teacher.
	You are the coach.
AC	You're the coach.
	He is the principal.
AC	He's the principal.
	She is a nurse.
AC	She's a nurse.

B1

*A **contraction** is the union of two words into one separated by an **apostrophe** ('). They are frequently used in English, especially when the subject is a pronoun.*

B2. Verb "to be": Negative Contractions (NC)

	I am not a teacher.
NC	I'm not a teacher.
	You are not a janitor.
NC	You're not a janitor.
NC	You aren't a janitor.
	He is not the principal.
NC	He's not the principal.
NC	He isn't the principal.

B2 - B3

*In negative sentences with the verb "to be", **negative contractions** can be done two ways, except when the subject is I.*

B3. Verb "to be": Negative Contractions (NC)

	She is not a secretary.
NC	She's not a secretary.
NC	She isn't a secretary.
	We are not counselors.
NC	We're not counselors.
NC	We aren't counselors.
	They are not nurses.
NC	They're not nurses.
NC	They aren't nurses.

B4. Question word: "where"

Where is the teacher?
She is **in the classroom.**

Where are the students?
They are **on the playground.**

Where is the janitor?
He is **in the hall.**

Where is the boy?
He is **in the library.**

B4 - B5

The question word "where" is used to find out the place where someone or something is. We answer the question identifying the place.

B5. Question word: "where"

Where is the nurse?
She is **in the clinic.**

Where is the principal?
He is **in the office.**

Where are the boys?
They are **in the auditorium.**

Where are the teachers?
They are **in the cafeteria.**

B6. Verb "to have": Present Tense

	I	have	a son.
	You	have	a mother.
Singular	He	**has**	an uncle.
	She	**has**	a sister.
	It	**has**	20 pages.
	We	have	nephews.
Plural	You	have	an aunt.
	They	have	a family.

B6

The verb "to have" is one of the most common verbs in English. It is an irregular verb. The form of the verb for the 3rd person singular he, she, it or a noun singular is has.

C1. Read and Listen to the dialog.

Who is your math teacher?
My math teacher is Mr. Finch.

How old is he?
He is twenty-seven years old.

Where is he now?
He's in the classroom.

Why aren't you there?
I am late.

Where is the principal?
He's in the main office.

Where is the coach?
He's on the playground.

Where are the students?
They're in the cafeteria.

Where is the janitor?
He is in the hall.

Where is the girl?
She's in the library.

Where is the nurse?
She's in her office.

C2. Read and Listen to the dialog.

Who is your English teacher?
My English teacher is Mr. Blake.

What is his first name?
His first name is Peter.

Is he old?
No, he is not old. He is young.

How old is he?
He's twenty-five years old.

Where is he?
He's in class with the students.

Why aren't you there?
I'm late.

Are you in trouble?
No, I am not. It's not my fault.

Where is the principal?
He is in his office.

Is he there alone?
No, he is with my counselor.

Where is your coach?
He is in the office also.

D1. principal / office

Is the principal in the auditorium?
No, he isn't in the auditorium.

Where is he?
He's in his office.

D2. counselor / playground

Is the counselor in the classroom?
No, he isn't in the classroom.

Where is he?
He's on the playground.

D3. Greg & Paul / cafeteria

Are Greg and Paul in the gymnasium?
No, they aren't in the gymnasium.

Where are they?
They're in the cafeteria.

D4. teacher / classroom

Is the teacher in the patio?
No, he isn't in the patio.

Where is he?
He's in the classroom.

Filling out a form

1. First name
2. Surnames
3. Father's name
4. Mother's name
5. Date of birth: Month / Day / Year
6. Country of birth
7. Nationality
8. Address
9. State
10. Zip Code

For the English audio pronunciations and written native language translations of **section E,** please go to:

www.basicesl.com

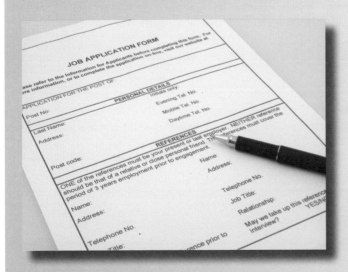

Application Forms

Information Forms

End of the **oral exercises** for lesson 4.

You can find additional exercises in sections D, F & G at Basic ESL Online.

Please continue with the **written exercises** for this lesson in **section H.**

Lesson

4

H1. Make contractions.

1. **She is** the coach.	*She's the coach.*
2. **I am** a student.	
3. **They are** in the hall.	
4. **We are** janitors.	
5. **Mary is** in the cafeteria.	
6. **Henry is** in the clinic.	
7. **You are** in the patio.	
8. **He is** in the restroom.	
9. **It is** in the library.	
10. **She is** in the office.	
11. **I am** in the playground.	
12. **You are** nice.	
13. **It is** good.	
14. **They are** polite.	

H2. Make the sentence negative. Then make contractions.

1. She is a teacher.

   *She **is not** a teacher.*
   ***She's not** a teacher.*
   *She **isn't** a teacher.*

2. You are the secretary.

   _____

   _____

   _____

3. They are students.

   _____

   _____

   _____

4. It is not your fault.

   _____

   _____

   _____

5. We are on the playground.

   _____

   _____

   _____

6. I am in the auditorium.

   _____

   _____

   _____

7. He is the coach.

   _____

   _____

   _____

H3. Follow the example.

1.   sister / classroom

gym

Where is your sister?
  She's in the gym.
  She isn't in the classroom.

2.   boys / playground

classroom

_____

_____

_____

3.   janitor / office

hall

_____

_____

_____

4.   students / cafeteria

auditorium

_____

_____

_____

5.   Fred / restroom

patio

_____

_____

_____

H4. Write the opposite.

1. short　　*tall*
2. rich　　_____
3. sad　　_____
4. old　　_____
5. married　　_____
6. thin　　_____

7. brother　　_____
8. father　　_____
9. nephew　　_____
10. cousin　　_____
11. son　　_____
12. uncle　　_____

H5. Change **Mary** for **Mary and Susan**.

Mary is a student. She's tall and beautiful. She's 13 years old. Her nationality is French. She comes from France. She loves this country.

She's very happy in the school. Her teacher is Mrs. Gonzalez. **Mary** speaks French and English. She sits in my English class. I study with my friend **Mary.**

Mary and Susan are students. _____
_____
_____
_____
_____
_____
_____
_____
_____
_____
_____
_____

Lesson #5

School Subjects

Index

Audio & Translations

 English Audio available online for sections A-E.

 Translations in various Languages available online for Sections A, B, and E.

www.BasicESL.com

1. math

2. music

3. spelling

4. art

5. computers

6. science

7. English

8. geography

9. physics

10. social studies

11. physical education

12. biology

13. Spanish

14. class

$$2 - 2 = 0$$

15. subtraction

$$2 + 2 = 4$$

16. addition

$$2 / 2 = 1$$

17. division

$$2 \times 2 = 4$$

18. multiplication

19. Chinese

20. French

21. German

Other Vocabulary

1.	n	grade
2.	n	language
3.	n	mistake
4.	n	writing
5.	adj	difficult
6.	adj	easy
7.	adj	correct
8.	adj	equal
9.	v	multiply

10.	v	practice
11.	v	subtract
12.	v	understand
13.	v	add
14.	v	answer
15.	v	divide
16.	v	enjoy
17.	adv	also
18.	pre	with

For the audio pronunciations and written translations of **Sections A and B,** please go to:

www.basicesl.com

Looking for Bilingual Dictionaries?
You can find a large selection at:

www.bilingualdictionaries.com

B1. Verbs: Negative (N) Statements

ⓘ

	I learn music.
N	I **do not learn** Spanish.
	You learn art.
N	You **do not learn** math.
	He learns science.
N	He **does not learn** spelling.
	She learns languages.
N	She **does not learn** geography.

B2. Verbs: Negative Statements (N)

	We **understand** history.
N	We **do not understand** science.
	I **know** geography.
N	I **do not know** math.
	My teacher **explains** art.
N	He **does not explain** homework.
	Peter **speaks** English.
N	He **does not speak** French.

B1 - B2

Except with the verb "to be", verbs form negative sentences in the present tense with the words "do not" or "does not" before the verb. "Does" is used when the subject is he, she, it, or a noun singular. In this case, the verb form loses the "-s" that shows in the affirmative form.

B3. Verbs: Negative Contractions (NC)

ⓘ

	Jane writes in Spanish.
NC	She **does not** write in English.
NC	She **doesn't** write in English.
	John plays at home.
NC	He **does not** play at school.
NC	He **doesn't** play at school.
	Lucy likes math.
NC	She **does not** like art.
NC	She **doesn't** like art.

B3

The words "do not" and "does not" can be contracted into "don't" and "doesn't."

B4. Verbs: Negative Contractions (NC)

	I **do not** live in Mexico.
NC	I **don't** live in Mexico.
	You **do not** come from Spain.
NC	You **don't** come from Spain.
	He **does not** love his sister.
NC	He **doesn't** love his sister.
	She **does not** learn science
NC	She **doesn't** learn science.

B4

*The words "**do not**" and "**does not**" can be contracted into "**don't**" and "**doesn't**."*

B5. Math Operations

addition
$2 + 2 = 4$
Two **plus** two equals four.

subtraction
$2 - 0 = 2$
Two **minus** zero equals two.

multiplication
$2 \times 3 = 6$
Two **times** three equals six.

division
$10 / 2 = 5$
Ten **divided by** 2 equals five.

B6. Math Operations

multiplication
$3 \times 3 = 9$
Three **multiplied by** three equals nine.

subtraction
$11 - 11 = 0$
Eleven **minus** eleven equals zero.

addition
$4 + 2 = 6$
Four **plus** two equals six.

division
$20 / 4 = 5$
Twenty **divided by** 4 equals five.

C1. Read and Listen to the story of Pat.

Pat **enjoys** art and music. She also **learns** geography with her teacher Mrs. Brown. Pat **loves** her teacher. The name of her teacher **is** Ann. She **is** from Mexico. She is twenty-three years old and she **has** a big family.

Pat **is** smart. Her writing **is** very good. She also **speaks** correct English. Besides, English, she **learns** Spanish and French at school. She **does not speak** French well. Her favorite subjects **are** spelling and foreign languages. She **likes** art also. She **does not like** music.

She **has** good grades in history and math. She **does not have** good grades in French. Her friend Lucy **likes** social studies and sports. Her coach Carol **is** her favorite teacher.

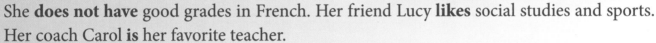

C1. Read and Listen to the story of Pat and I.

Pat and I **enjoy** art and music. We also **learn** geography with our teacher Mrs. Brown. Pat and I **love** our teacher. The name of our teacher **is** Anna. She **is** from Mexico. She **is** twenty-three years old and she **has** a big family.

Pat and I **are** smart. Our writing **is** very good. We also **speak** correct English. Besides English, we **learn** Spanish and French at school. We **do not speak** French well. Our favorite subjects **are** spelling and foreign languages. We **like** music also. We **do not like** art.

We **have** good grades in history and math. We **do not have** good grades in French. Our friend Lucy **likes** social studies and sports. Our coach Mrs. Carol **is** our favorite teacher.

D1. Joe / like / music

Joe **likes** math.
He **does not** like music.

Is music easy?
No, it is not. It is difficult.

D2. sisters / enjoy / languages

My sisters **enjoy** art.
They **do not enjoy** languages.

Are languages easy?
No, they are not. They are difficult.

D3. Sara / learn / spelling

Sara **learns** geography.
She **does not learn** spelling.

Is spelling easy?
No, it is not. It is difficult.

D4. students / speak / Spanish

The students **speak** English.
They **do not speak** Spanish.

Is Spanish easy?
No, it is not. It is difficult.

Exclamations

1. **Good gracious!**
2. **What a pity!**
3. **What a surprise!**
4. **What a relief!**
5. **What a shame!**
6. **How awful!**
7. **How disgusting!**
8. **How scary!**
9. **How wonderful!**
10. **How stupid!**

For the English audio pronunciations and written native language translations of **section E,** please go to:

www.basicesl.com

What a shame!

How stupid!

End of the **oral exercises** for lesson 5.

You can find additional exercises in sections D, F & G at Basic ESL Online.

Please continue with the **written exercises** for this lesson in **section H**.

H1. Complete with **do** or **does**.

1. I   *do*   not study French.
2. She   _____ not enjoy music.
3. Nancy   _____ not speak English.
4. You   _____ not study science.
5. The student _____ not like geography.
6. The students _____ not learn typing.
7. He   _____ not write the exercises.

H2. Make the sentence **negative**.

1. I know geography.   *I do not know* _____ geography.
2. You know science.   _____ science.
3. He knows art.   _____ art.
4. She knows spelling.   _____ spelling.
5. My brothers know math.   _____ math.
6. We know music.   _____ music.
7. They know history.   _____ history.

H3. Make the sentence negative.

1. Lucy **writes** in English.   *Lucy **does not write** in English.*
   Her pen **is** beautiful.   *Her pen **is not** beautiful.*

2. We **draw** pictures.
   The pictures **are** nice.

3. Ray **enjoys** the class.
   The class **is** short.

4. He **understands** music.
   Music **is** nice.

5. I **study** the lessons.
   The lessons **are** easy.

6. She **loves** her name.
   Her name **is** pretty.

H4. Write the math operation.

1. $3 + 3 = 6$ *Three plus three equals six.*

2. $4 \times 2 = 8$

3. $5 - 0 = 5$

4. $6 / 2 = 3$

5. $12 - 1 = 11$

6. $2 \times 10 = 20$

7. $13 - 4 = 9$

H5. Follow the example.

1. Kathy (12) / likes / art

social studies

How old is Kathy?
She is twelve years old.

*Kathy **likes** social studies.*
*She **does not like** art.*

2. girls (9) / practice / music

Physical Ed.

_____
_____
_____
_____

3. boys (11) / love / math

science

_____
_____
_____
_____

4. Rachel (10) / write / English

Spanish

_____
_____
_____
_____

5. nephews (8) / play / home

school

_____
_____
_____
_____

H6. Write the same story in the **negative form**.

Pat is my friend. She is 12 years old. She **enjoys** art and music. She also **learns** geography with her teacher Mrs. Brown. Pat **loves** her teacher. She is from England. She is twenty-three years old.

Pat is smart. Her writing is good. She **speaks** good English. She **learns** Spanish and French at school. Spelling is her favorite subject.

She **has** good grades in history and math. Her friend Lucy **likes** social studies and sports. Her coach Carol is her favorite teacher.

Pat is not my friend. _____

_____

_____

_____

_____

_____

_____

_____

_____

_____

_____

_____

_____

_____

_____

_____

_____

_____

_____

_____

_____

_____

_____

Lesson #6

School Objects

Index

Audio & Translations

English Audio available online for sections A-E.

Translations in various Languages available online for Sections A, B, and E.

www.BasicESL.com

1. eraser

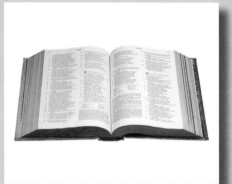

2. book

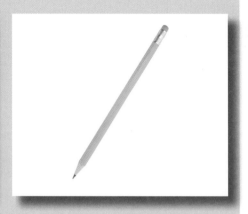

3. pencil

4. envelope

5. ruler

6. pen

7. chair

8. notebook

9. ink

10. table

11. lamp

12. scissors

13. wastebasket

14. chalkboard

15. map

16. clock

17. desk

18. flag

19. glue

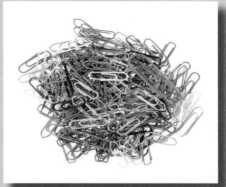

20. paper clip

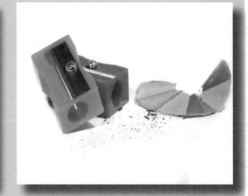

21. pencil sharpener

Other Vocabulary

1.	n	location	10.	v	shout
2.	n	pair	11.	v	use
3.	n	word	12.	v	want
4.	adj	all	13.	v	wish
5.	adj	big	14.	adv	here
6.	v	desire	15.	pro	what
7.	v	inform	16.	pro	who
8.	v	punish	17.	pre	except
9.	v	return	18.	pre	of

For the audio pronunciations and written translations of **Sections A and B**, please go to:

www.BasicESL.com

Looking for Bilingual Dictionaries?
You can find a large selection at:

www.bilingualdictionaries.com

A - Picture Vocabulary

B1. Verbs: Present Tense: Questions (Q)

They love their mother.

Q   **Do they** love their mother?

You love Mary.

Q   **Do you** love Mary?

He love**s** his father

Q   **Does he** love his father?

She love**s** her brother.

Q   **Does she** love her brother?

B2. Verbs: Present Tense: Questions (Q)

She **erases** the mistakes.

Q   **Does** she **erase** the mistakes?

Greg **asks** questions.

Q   **Does** Greg **ask** questions?

You **answer** the questions.

Q   **Do** you **answer** the questions?

We **correct** the exercises.

Q   **Do** we **correct** the exercises?

B3. Verb "to have": Verb Form: Present Tense

I	**have**	a flag.
You	**have**	a map.
He	**has**	a book.
She	**has**	a desk.
It (the school)	**has**	a clock.
We	**have**	pens.
You (pl)	**have**	notebooks.
They	**have**	chairs.

B1 - B2

In English, questions in the present tense begin with "do" or "does" followed by the subject of the verb. In questions, the verb form is the same for all subjects.

B3

The verb "to have" is one of the most common verbs in English. It is an irregular verb. The form of the verb for the 3rd person singular, he, she, it or a noun singular is has.

B4. Verb "to have": Negative Statements

I **have** a flag.
You **do not have** a map.

He **has** a book.
He **does not have** a pen.

She **has** a desk.
She **does not have** a chair.

We **have** pencils.
We **do not have** erasers.

B4 - B5

The verb "to have" is one the most common verbs in English. In affirmative sentences this verb uses the form "has" when the subject of the sentences is he, she, it, or a noun singular.

In negative sentences and in questions the verb form "to have" is the same for all subjects.

B5. Verb "to have": Questions and Answers

Do you **have** envelopes?
Yes, I **have** envelopes.
How many envelopes do you **have**?
I **have** 5 envelopes.

Does Frank **have** rulers?
Yes, he **has** rulers.
How many rulers does he **have**?
He **has** 7 rulers.

B6. Question Words: "who, what"

Who is this?
This **my cousin.**

What is his **name?**
His name is **John.**

What is he **like?**
He is **tall** and **handsome.**

How many friends does he have?
He has at least **9** friends.

B6

Questions words are those that we use to ask questions with the purpose of obtaining definite information. This information can be about the age, the name, the quantity, the description, the identification of people or things, the way we are or act, etc. They are especially important in conversations.

C1. Read and Listen to the dialog.

What are these?
These are pens and pencils.

What is that?
That is a pair of scissors.

How many books do you have?
I have eight books.

How many rulers does Sara have?
She has two rulers.

Do the students have desks?
Yes, they have.

Do they have lamps on the desks?
No, they don't have lamps.

What does the school have?
It has a clock.

Does it have a flag also?
Yes, it has a flag.

Who has the big table?
The teacher has the big table.

Do the students like the school?
Yes, they like the school.

C2. Read and Listen to the Story.

Tom and I are good friends. We are in the same geography class. In our class, we have a map of the United States. It is a big map.

Tom and I are smart. Our writing is very good. We have two workbooks. We write with a pencil in our thin workbooks. We correct the mistakes with an eraser. We use the same rulers, pens and pencils.

Our grades are good in history and math. We enjoy art and music. Science is our favorite subject.

D1. Mike (8) / map

What does Mike have?
He has rulers.

How many rulers does he have?
He has 8 rulers.

Does he have a map also?
No, he does not have a map.

D2. Alice and Sara (20) / desk

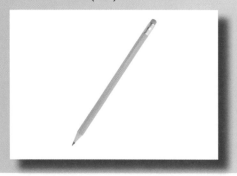

What do Alice and Sara have?
They have pens.

How many pens do they have?
They have 20 pens.

Do they have a desk also?
No, they do not have a desk.

D3. Helen (11) / scissors

What does Helen have?
She has pencils.

How many pencils does she have?
She has 11 pencils.

Does she have a pair of scissors also?
No, she does not have a pair of scissors.

D4. students (13) / flag

What do the students have?
They have envelopes.

How many envelopes do they have?
They have 13 envelopes.

Do they have a flag also?
No, they do not have a flag.

Saying good bye.

1. Good bye.
2. Bye.
3. See you.
4. See you soon.
5. See you in a minute.
6. See you tomorrow.
7. See you then.
8. See you later.
9. Good night.
10. Until tomorrow.

For the English audio pronunciations and written native language translations of **section E,** please go to:

www.basicesl.com

See you soon.

Good Bye.

End of the **oral exercises** for lesson 6.

You can find additional exercises in sections D, F & G at Basic ESL Online.

Please continue with the **written exercises** for this lesson in **section H.**

Lesson

6

H1. Change to Questions.

#	Sentence	Question	
1.	You love your father.	*Do you love*	your father?
2.	He loves his sister.	_____	his sister?
3.	She loves her mother.	_____	her mother?
4.	We love our son.	_____	our son?
5.	They love their uncles.	_____	their uncles?
6.	Greg asks questions.	_____	questions?
7.	Tom shouts in class.	_____	in class?
8.	She speaks English.	_____	English?
9.	The class begins now.	_____	now?
10.	We understand math.	_____	math?
11.	Tony knows geography.	_____	geography?
12.	Jane draws pictures.	_____	pictures?
13.	They write in English.	_____	in English?
14.	We use erasers.	_____	erasers?
15.	Henry wants a lamp.	_____	a lamp?
16.	I have a desk.	_____	a desk?

H2. Answer the questions.

1. Do you **ask** questions?

   *Yes, I **ask** questions.*
   *No, I **do not ask** questions.*

2. Do they **shout** in class?

   _____

   _____

3. Does Mary **speak** English?

   _____

   _____

4. Does the class **begin** now?

   _____

   _____

5. Do they **understand** math?

   _____

   _____

6. Does Tony **know** history?

   _____

   _____

7. Do you **draw** pictures?

   _____

   _____

8. Does she **write** in Spanish?

   _____

   _____

9. We **use** erasers.

   _____

   _____

H3. Circle the correct answer.

1. I write with a . . .   erase   calculator   pen   blackboard

2. I write on the . . .   pen   pencil   ruler   blackboard

3. . . . is a liquid object.   clip   table   ink   desk

4. We cut paper with . . .   stapler   scissors   clock   wastebasket

5. We use an eraser on the . . . clip   lamp   notebook envelope

6. . . . is a sticky object.   glue   map   flag   chair

H4. Multiple choice. Select the correct answer.

1. They want **an** eraser.   *a, they,* **an**

2. Lisa _____ music.   enjoy, loves, take

3. Lisa does not _____ art.   enjoys, loves, take

4. We _____ learn math.   do not, does not

5. She _____ in the office.   isn't, love, aren't

6. The flags _____ big.   isn't, love, aren't

7. Fred_____ a desk.   has, reads, have

8. _____ old is the teacher?   Is, How, He

9. My brother does not _____ typing.   writes, loves, study

10. Tony _____ English.   learn, learns, to learn

H5. Follow the example.

1. Mike / blackboard

    ruler

    What does Mike have?

    He has a ruler.

    He does not have a blackboard.

2. boys / tables

    envelopes

3. teacher / flag

    wastebasket

4. students / notebooks

    lamps

5. you / book

    crayon

Chapter 3
The House

Lesson 7: Places in the house
Lesson 8: The Kitchen
Lesson 9: Bedroom - Bathroom

What to do in each section of every lesson...

A - Vocabulary Study

Section A includes the vocabulary that will be used throughout the lesson. Learning new vocabulary is basic to learning a new language.

Read the vocabulary several times.
If you are on Basic ESL Online:
Listen to the **English audio pronunciation**.
View the **native language translations** of the vocabulary.

Listen and read the vocabulary until you can understand the vocabulary without looking at the words.

B - Sentence Structure

Section B teaches students basic English sentences using the vocabulary in section A.

Read and **study** the sentences.
If you are on Basic ESL Online:
Listen to the **English audio pronunciation**.
View the **native language translations** of the sentences.
View the **grammar concepts** by clicking on the **information button** .

Repeat the sentences as many times as needed. Continue to the next section once you can **understand** the sentences without looking at them.

C - Listening Exercises

Read the story or dialog several times.
If you are on Basic ESL Online, **listen** to the story or dialog while reading it several times.

Once you are familiar with the story or dialog, try to see if you can **understand** it by only listening without reading.

D - Conversation Exercises

Read the conversation dialogs several times.
If you are on Basic ESL Online, **listen** to the dialogs until you can understand them without looking at them.

Finally, try to **speak** the conversation dialogs by only looking at the pictures and key words.

E - Common Phrases

Many of the **common phrases** that are presented in this section are frequently used by the native English speakers in their everyday life.

Read the common phrases several times.
If you are on Basic ESL Online, **listen** to the common phrases while reading. **Listen** as many times as needed until you can understand the common phrases without looking at the sentences.

H - Written Exercises

The written exercises provide an opportunity to test what you learned in the lesson. You can never be sure of knowing something unless you can put it in writing.

You can check your answers by going to the **Answer Key Section** in the back of the workbook.

For information regarding **Basic ESL Online,** please visit **www.basicesl.com.**
Audio Pronunciaton of English & Native Language Translations.

Lesson #7

Places in the House

Index

Audio & Translations

English Audio available online for sections A-E.

Translations in various Languages available online for Sections A, B, and E.

www.BasicESL.com

1. attic

2. backyard

3. bathroom

4. basement

5. ceiling

6. bedroom

7. fence

8. driveway

9. garage

10. gate

11. kitchen

12. living room

13. porch

14. patio

15. roof

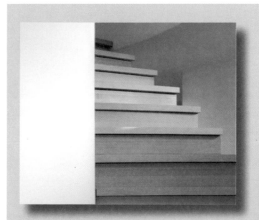

16. stairs

17. hall

18. window

19. door

20. balcony

Other Vocabulary

1.	n	bell	10.	v	enter
2.	n	apartment	11.	v	open
3.	adj	second	12.	v	watch
4.	v	read	13.	v	prefer
5.	v	care	14.	adv	upstairs
6.	v	close	15.	adv	downstairs
7.	v	sit	16.	adv	too
8.	v	knock	17.	pre	after
9.	v	rest	18.	pre	on

For the audio pronunciations and written translations of **Sections A and B,** please go to:

www.basicesl.com

B1. Verb "to be": Questions

She **is** in the hall.
Q **Is** she in the hall?

You **are** on the stairs.
Q **Are** you on the stairs?

The girl **is** in the bathroom.
Q **Is** the girl in the bathroom?

The boy **is** on the roof.
Q **Is** the boy on the roof?

B1 - B2 - B3

*In **questions** with the verb "to be", we do not use "**do**" or "**does**". We form questions by placing the verb "to be" **before** the subject.*

B2. Verb "to be": Affirmative and Negative Answers

Is Mary in the kitchen?
A Yes, **she is** in the kitchen.
N No, **she is not** in the kitchen.

Are you in the bedroom?
A Yes, **I am** in the bedroom.
N No, **I am not** in the bedroom.

Is Tony in the garage?
A Yes, **he is** in the garage.
N No, **he is not** in the garage.

B3. Verb "to be": Affirmative and Negative Answers

Are the boys in the backyard?
A Yes, **they are** in the backyard.
N No, **they are not** in the backyard.

Is your aunt on the porch?
A Yes, **she is** on the porch.
N No, **she is not** on the porch.

Is your uncle in the basement?
A Yes, **he is** in the basement.
N No, **he is not** in the basement.

B4. Comparing Questions

Do you **have** three bedrooms?
Are the bedrooms upstairs?

Does Lucy **open** the windows?
Are the windows big?

Does dad **rest** on the porch?
Is the porch small?

Does Peter **knock** on the door?
Is the door strong?

B4 - B5

*When comparing questions with the verb "to be" and questions with other verbs, you will notice that "**do**" or "**does**" is not used with the verb "**to be**". It is used with other verbs.*

B5. Comparing Questions

Do you **close** the gate?
Is the gate made of wood?

Does mom **prefer** high ceilings?
Are the ceilings high?

Do you **clean** the bathrooms?
Are the bathrooms clean?

Does she **sleep** in the living room?
Is the living room large?

B6. Review: Possessive Adjectives

I buy **my** books.
You buy **your** pens.

Tony buys **his** pencils.
We buy **our** maps.

They buy **their** scissors.
The school buys **its** flag.

She buys **her** notebooks.
Paul and **I** buy **our** lamps.

B6

Possessive adjectives indicate to whom something belongs. This exercise shows the relation between the subject pronoun and the corresponding possessive adjective when the thing or person possessed belongs to the subject.

C1. Read and Listen to the story.

My family lives in a big house. The house is not too old. It's only ten years old. It is a beautiful house. It has a patio and a porch in front of the house. My family enjoys the backyard of the house. My sister and I play in the backyard. My mom likes to sit on the porch and read books. My dad likes to work in the backyard.

Our house has five bedrooms and three bathrooms. One bathroom and one of the bedrooms are downstairs. The other four bedrooms and two bathrooms are upstairs. My parents have a master bedroom with its own bathroom inside.

C2. Read and Listen to the dialog.

Does Henry live in a house or apartment?
He lives in a house with his family.

How many bedrooms does the house have?
It has three bedrooms and two bathrooms. Two bedrooms and one bathroom are upstairs on the second floor. The other bathroom and bedroom are downstairs.

Where is Henry now?
He is on the roof.
He likes to be on the roof or in the attic.
He does not like to be in the basement.

D1. Mike / bedroom / study

Is Mike in the living room?
No, he is not in the living room.

Where is he?
He is in the bedroom.

Does he study in the bedroom?
No, he does not study there.

D2. Mary / patio / rest

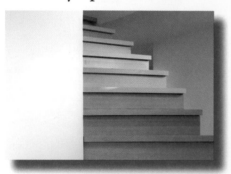

Is Mary on the stairs?
No, she is not on the stairs.

Where is she?
She is on the patio.

Does she rest on the patio?
No, she does not rest there.

D3. nephews / kitchen / watch TV

Are the nephews in the basement?
No, they are not in the basement.

Where are they?
They are in the kitchen.

Do they watch TV in the kitchen?
No, they do not watch TV there.

D4. you / garage / play

Are you in the bedroom?
No, I am not in the bedroom.

Where are you?
I am in the garage.

Do you play in the garage?
No, I do not play there.

Expressing feelings

1. How do you feel?
2. I feel great.
3. I feel so-so.
4. I feel terrible.
5. I feel sad.
6. I feel awful.
7. I feel upset.
8. I feel worried.
9. I feel stressed out.
10. I feel very happy.

For the English audio pronunciations and written native language translations of **section E,** please go to:

www.basicesl.com

I feel stressed.

I feel worried.

End of the **oral exercises** for lesson 7.

You can find additional exercises in sections D, F & G at Basic ESL Online.

Please continue with the **written exercises** for this lesson in **section H.**

Lesson 7

H1. Change the statements to questions.

1. **Mary** is in the kitchen.
2. The windows are small.
3. The balcony is big.
4. You are in the balcony.
5. The desks are in the attic.
6. Henry is in the garage.
7. The girls are in the hall.
8. The house is beautiful.
9. The doors are pretty.
10. The hall is long.
11. The ceiling is high.
12. The porch is nice.
13. The apartment is small.
14. The attic is upstairs.

*Is **Mary** in the kitchen?*
_____
_____
_____
_____
_____
_____
_____
_____
_____
_____
_____
_____
_____

H2. Change the statements to questions.

1. The doorbell is small.
   The boys ring the bell.

   Is the doorbell small?
   Do the boys ring the bell?

2. He scrubs the floors.
   The floors are dirty.

   _____
   _____

3. The stove is too big.
   We need a new stove.

   _____
   _____

4. The doors are heavy.
   Frank closes the doors.

   _____
   _____

5. The stairs are pretty.
   You love the stairs.

   _____
   _____

6. The boy is on the roof.
   He likes to be on the roof.

   _____
   _____

7. The sofa is new.
   Mom sits on the sofa.

   _____
   _____

8. The windows are small.
   Henry opens the windows.

   _____
   _____

9. Jane sleeps on the bed.
   The bed is big.

   _____
   _____

H3. Make the sentences plural.

1. The boy is tall.
2. The nephew is here.
3. I use a notebook.
4. She rests on the sofa.
5. The girl wants a pen.
6. You prefer a lamp.
7. My friend sits here.
8. He reads a book.
9. It is upstairs.
10. I am downstairs.

The boys are tall.

H4. Ask the questions corresponding to these answers.

1. Tom is in **the classroom.**
2. He is **10 years** old.
3. He is **handsome.**
4. He is a **student.**
5. He has **20** pencils.
6. His sister is **here.**
7. **She** is tall.
8. She is **beautiful.**
9. Her name is **Liz.**
10. She speaks **French.**
11. She has **two** cousins.

Where is Tom?

H5. Follow the example.

1. Tom-Alex / basement

roof

Are Tom and Alex on the roof?
No, they are not on the roof.

Where are they?
They are in the basement.

2. Cynthia / garage

balcony

3. they / kitchen

hall

4. Fred / attic

backyard

5. Liz-you / hall

porch

Lesson #8

The Kitchen

Index

Audio & Translations

 English Audio available online for sections A-E.

 Translations in various Languages available online for Sections A, B, and E.

www.BasicESL.com

1. blender

2. cup

3. dishwasher

4. dining table

5. fork

6. glass

7. kettle

8. knife

9. napkin

10. pan

11. plate

12. refrigerator

13. spoon

14. saucepan

15. tablecloth

16. stove

17. tray

18. toaster

19. dish

20. apron

21. microwave

13. sink

14. saucer

15. shelf

Other Vocabulary

1.	n	cabinet	**7.**	adj	clean	**13.**	v	scrub
2.	n	center	**8.**	adj	dirty	**14.**	v	serve
3.	n	counter	**9.**	v	wash	**15.**	v	stay
4.	n	drawer	**10.**	v	help	**16.**	v	touch
5.	adj	another	**11.**	v	need	**17.**	v	miss
6.	adj	huge	**12.**	v	place	**18.**	pre	above

B1. Irregular Plural of Nouns

Singular	Plural
brush	brushes
dish	dishes
mattress	mattresses
glass	glasses
porch	porches
church	churches
potato	potatoes
tomato	tomatoes

B1

As a rule, nouns form the plural by adding an "-s" to their singular form. There are few **exceptions** *depending on the ending of the noun.*

Nouns ending in **h, s, z, x, ch** *and* **o**, *add "-es".*

B2. Irregular Plural of Nouns

Singular	Plural
knife	knives
wife	wives
life	lives
shelf	shelves
half	halves
family	families
baby	babies

B2

Nouns ending in "-y", preceded by a consonant, form their plural by changing the **y** *into "-ies".*

Nouns ending in "-f" or "-fe" change to "-ves."

B3. Irregular Plural of Nouns

Singular	Plural
man	men
child	children
woman	women
foot	feet
tooth	teeth
mouse	mice
goose	geese

B3

Some nouns have different words in the plural form.

B4. Irregular Plural of Nouns

Singular	Plural
sheep	sheep
deer	deer
fish	fish
alumnus	alumni
stimulus	stimuli
crisis	crises
diagnosis	diagnoses

B4

Some nouns keep the same form in the singular and in the plural.

Irregular nouns ending in "-us" change to "-i".

Those ending in "-is" change to "-es".

B5. Possesive Adjectives (P.A.)

S.P.	Verb	P.A.	
I	love	**my**	son.
You	love	**your**	daughter.
He	loves	**his**	sister.
She	loves	**her**	brother.
We	love	**our**	father.
You	love	**your**	parents.
They	love	**their**	nephew.

B5 (Review)

Possessive adjectives indicate possession.

B6. English Punctuation Marks

?	question mark
!	exclamation mark
" "	quotation marks
,	comma
.	period
:	colon
;	semi-colon
–	hyphen
'	apostrophe

C1. Read and Listen to the story of Rose.

Rose likes my family. She prefers to stay at my house. She loves our kitchen. Our kitchen is big. It has a huge refrigerator, a dishwasher and a stove. Our kitchen also has many drawers and cabinets.

My mom keeps the spoons, forks and knives in one drawer. She keeps the napkins and the tablecloths in another drawer. The plates, glasses and cups are in one of the kitchen cabinets. The kettles, pans and trays are in another cabinet.

C2. Read and Listen to the dialog. (Review)

Who is your English teacher?
My English teacher is Mr. Blake.

What is his first name?
His first name is Peter.

Is he old?
No, he is not old. He is young.

How old is he?
He's twenty-five years old.

Where is he?
He's in class with the students.

Why aren't you there?
I'm late.

Are you in trouble?
No, I am not. It's not my fault.

Where is the principal?
He is in his office.

Is he there alone?
No, he is with my counselor.

Where is your coach?
He is in the office also.

D1. Mary

Mary has many glasses.

Does she need more glasses?
Yes, she needs more glasses.

How many more does she need?
She only needs one more glass.

D2. brothers

My brothers have many dishes.

Do they need more dishes?
Yes, they need more dishes.

How many more do they need?
They only needs one more dish.

D3. aunt

My aunt has many knives.

Does she need more knives?
Yes, she needs more knives.

How many more does she need?
She only needs one more knife.

D4. John

John has many trays.

Does he need more trays?
Yes, he needs more trays.

How many more does he need?
He only needs one more tray.

Time of day

1. What time is it?
2. It is 8:00.
3. What time does school start?
4. It starts at 8:30.
5. What time does the bus arrive?
6. It arrives at 8:10.
7. What time does it leave?
8. It leaves at 8:15.
9. Do I have enough time?
10. I'm afraid not.

For the English audio pronunciations and written native language translations of **section E**, please go to:

www.basicesl.com

What time is it?

Do I have enough time?

End of the **oral exercises** for lesson 8.

You can find additional exercises in sections D, F & G at Basic ESL Online.

Please continue with the **written exercises** for this lesson in **section H**.

Lesson

8

H1. Make the nouns plural.

1. child   *children*

2. dish   _____

3. family   _____

4. foot   _____

5. man   _____

6. mouse   _____

7. potato   _____

8. sheep   _____

9. tooth   _____

10. woman   _____

11. church   _____

12. goose   _____

13. diagnosis   _____

14. brush   _____

15. tomato   _____

16. deer   _____

17. garage   _____

18. half   _____

19. knife   _____

20. life   _____

21. mattress   _____

22. porch   _____

23. shelf   _____

24. tray   _____

25. watch   _____

26. baby   _____

27. fish   _____

28. alumnus   _____

29. glass   _____

H2. Make the sentence plural.

1. The boy likes the cup.
   The blender is old.

   The boys like the cups.
   The blenders are old.

2. The lady is a teacher.
   She works in a library.

3. The door is heavy.
   He knocks on the door.

4. I watch the child.
   He sleeps on the sofa.

5. The man needs a glass.
   His glass is broken.

6. The self is dirty.
   It is near the baby.

7. My knife is not sharp.
   I need a new knife.

8. Your brush is long.
   You like a short brush.

9. The church is pretty.
   He likes a pretty church.

H3. Make correct sentences with the correct form of the verb.

1. Mary - music - learn   *Mary learns music.*
2. Spanish - they -speak?
3. our - love - he - kitchen
4. Frank - dishes - clean?
5. have - Tom - sister - two.
6. are - classroom - we - same.
7. do - Spanish - speak - we - not.
8. the - like - boys - blender?
9. like - not - they - blender.
10. brush - are - where - new?

H4. Write the math operations.

1. $2 \times 3 = 9$ *Two times three equals nine.*
2. $7 + 5 = 12$
3. $13 - 9 = 4$
4. $18 / 6 = 3$
5. $20 - 14 = 6$

H5. Make the subject and the object of the verb singular.

1. The knives are sharp.   *The knife is sharp.*
2. We have big families.
3. The porches are beautiful.
4. You have glasses.
5. They read in the churches.
6. The wives are with the babies.
7. Our lives are happy.
8. We want tomatoes.

H6. Follow the example.

1.   Jane / need

knife

> ***What does Jane need?***
> She needs knives sometimes.
>
> ***How many does she need now?***
> She only needs one knife now.

2.   mom / need

mattress

_____

_____

_____

_____

3.   women / need

toothbrush

_____

_____

_____

_____

4.   Tony / need

mouse

_____

_____

_____

_____

5.   kitchen / need

shelf

_____

_____

_____

_____

Lesson #9

The Bedroom & Bathroom

Index

Audio & Translations

 English Audio available online for sections A-E.

 Translations in various Languages available online for Sections A, B, and E.

www.BasicESL.com

1. bathtub

2. bed

3. bedspread

4. blanket

5. closet

6. comb

7. drapes

8. dresser

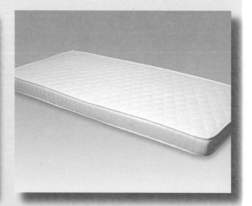

9. mattress

10. mirror

11. pillow

12. pillowcase

13. sheet

14. razor

15. shower

16. toilet

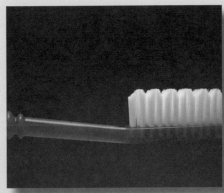

17. toothbrush

18. washstand

19. shower head

20. faucet

21. toothpaste

Other Vocabulary

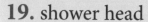

1.	n	soap		10.	v	keep
2.	adj	nice		11.	v	prefer
3.	adj	hard		12.	v	hang
4.	adj	soft		13.	v	match
5.	adj	alone		14.	v	look
6.	adj	surprised		15.	v	fold
7.	v	like		16.	v	sleep
8.	v	clean		17.	v	wash
9.	v	use		18.	adv	really

For the pronunciation and translation of **the sections A and B,** you can go online at:

www.basicesl.com

B1. Verb "to be": Negative Questions (NQ)

	The dresser **is not** nice.
NQ	**Is** the dresser **not** nice?
NQ	**Isn't** the dresser nice?

	The mirrors **are not** big.
NQ	**Are** the mirrors **not** big?
NQ	**Aren't** the mirrors big?

	The sheets **are not** clean.
NQ	**Are** the sheets **not** clean?
NQ	**Aren't** the sheets clean?

B2. Verb "to be": Negative Questions (NQ)

	The bed **is not** strong.
NQ	**Is** the bed **not** strong?
NQ	**Isn't** the bed strong?

	The razor **is not** sharp.
NQ	**Is** the razor **not** sharp?
NQ	**Isn't** the razor sharp?

	The combs **are not** hard.
NQ	Are the combs **not** hard?
NQ	**Aren't** the combs hard?

B3. Verb "to be": Negative Questions (NQ)

	The faucet **is not** new.
NQ	**Is** the faucet **not** new?
NQ	**Isn't** the faucet new?

	The drapes **are not** heavy.
NQ	**Are** the drapes **not** heavy?
NQ	**Aren't** the drapes heavy?

	The bathtub **is not** dirty.
NQ	**Is** the bathtub **not** dirty?
NQ	**Isn't** the bathtub dirty?

B1 - B2 - B3

In English **questions** in the negative form are not really questions denying something. They are used by the speaker when he is expecting or suspecting an affirmative answer. The answer to these questions can be affirmative or negative.

With the verb **"to be"**, negative questions are formed **two** ways: either with contractions or without contractions.

B4. Verbs: Comparing Negative Sentences

The shower **is not** old.
It **does not** work.

The pillows **are not** pretty.
They **do not** match the bedspread.

The closet **is not** big.
It **does not** have much room.

The blankets **are not** heavy.
They **do not** weigh much.

B5. Math Operations

B5 (Review)

addition	$2 + 2 = 4$
	Two **plus** two equals four.
subtraction	$2 - 0 = 2$
	Two **minus** zero equals two.
multiplication	$2 \times 3 = 6$
	Two **times** three equals six.
division	$10 / 2 = 5$
	Ten **divided by** 2 equals five.

B6. Questions: Verb "to be" and other verbs

B6 (Review)

Do you **have** three bedrooms?
Are the bedrooms upstairs?

Does Lucy **open** the windows?
Are the windows big?

Does dad **rest** on the porch?
Is the porch small?

Does Peter **knock** on the door?
Is the door strong?

C1. Read and Listen to the story of Jane.

Jane is a friend of my sister Mary. She is 16 years old. She speaks English. She does not practice Spanish at her home.

Jane prefers to stay in my house. She loves my kitchen and my bedroom. The bedroom looks nice. It has beautiful drapes.

Jane makes my bed every day. She arranges the sheets, the bedspread, the pillows and the blanket. She hangs the clothes in the closet. She also cleans the mirror, the bathtub and the shower in the bathroom. Jane is really a good friend.

C2. Read and Listen to the dialog.

What are these?
These are pens and pencils.

What is that?
That is a pair of scissors.

How many books do you have?
I have eight books.

How many rulers does Sara have?
She has two rulers.

Do the students have desks?
Yes, they have.

Do they have lamps on the desks?
No, they don't have lamps.

What does the school have?
It has a clock.

Does it have a flag also?
Yes, it has a flag.

Who has the big table?
The teacher has the table.

Do the students like the school?
Yes, they like the school.

D1. Mary / use-hairbrush-hard

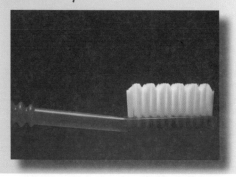

Does Mary use a toothbrush?
No, she doesn't use a toothbrush.

What does she use?
She uses a hairbrush.

Aren't hairbrushes hard?
No, they aren't hard. They are soft.

D2. nieces / want-bedspread-ugly

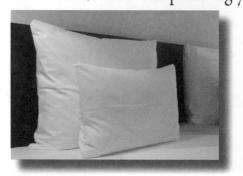

Do your nieces want pillows?
No, they don't want pillows.

What do they want?
They want a beadspread.

Aren't bedspreads ugly?
No, they aren't ugly. They are beautiful.

D3. John / clean-bed-light

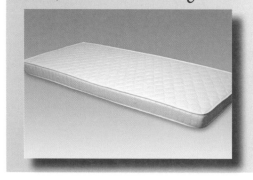

Does John clean the mattress?
No, he doesn't clean the mattress.

What does he clean?
He cleans the bed.

Aren't beds light weight?
No, they aren't light. They are heavy.

D4. girls / buy-combs-big

Do the girls buy razors?
No, they don't buy razors.

What do they buy?
They buy combs.

Aren't combs big?
No, they aren't big. They are small.

House Chores

1. What are your tasks at home?
2. I sweep the patio.
3. I take out the trash.
4. I dust the furniture.
5. I arrange the closet.
6. I mop the kitchen floor.
7. I make the beds.
8. I change the sheets.
9. I vacuum the carpet.
10. I scrub the pans.

For the English audio pronunciations and written native language translations of **section E,** please go to:

www.basicesl.com

I vacuum the carpet.

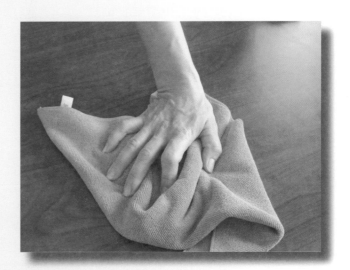

I dust the furniture.

End of the **oral exercises** for lesson 9.

You can find additional exercises in sections D, F & G at Basic ESL Online.

Please continue with the **written exercises** for this lesson in **section H**.

Lesson

9

H1. Make the sentence negative.

1.	The shower is beautiful.	*The shower is **not***	beautiful.
2.	Ann cleans the shower.		the shower.
3.	The sheets are clean.		clean.
4.	We wash the sheets.		the sheets.
5.	The bathtub is dirty.		dirty.
6.	Mom cleans the bathtub.		the bathtub.
7.	The blankets are nice.		nice.
8.	Sara folds the blankets.		the blankets.
9.	The mirrors are big.		big.
10.	I need new mirrors.		new mirrors.
11.	The drapes are new.		new.
12.	The pillows are small.		small.
13.	You need big pillows.		big pillows.
14.	The faucets are old.		old.
15.	We need other faucets.		other faucets.

H2. Change the negative sentences to questions.

1. Mark **is not** tall.

   *Is Mark **not** tall?*
   Isn't Mark tall?

2. The drapes **are not** clean.

   _____

   _____

3. The pillows **are not** ugly.

   _____

   _____

4. The toilet **is not** dirty.

   _____

   _____

5. John **is not** a bad boy.

   _____

   _____

6. The shower **is not** new.

   _____

   _____

7. The closets **are not** big.

   _____

   _____

8. This razor **is not** sharp.

   _____

   _____

9. The bedspread **is not** small.

   _____

   _____

H3. Circle the kitchen items.

1.	toothpaste	pillow	pan	fork
2.	comb	plate	knife	bed
3.	ink	glass	mirror	spoon
4.	stove	kettle	shower	faucet
5.	closet	microwave	toilet	cup
6.	armchair	blender	bathtub	toaster

H4. Make the subject and the object of the verb plural.

1. The knife is sharp.   *The knives are sharp.*
2. I have a big family. _____
3. The porch is beautiful. _____
4. You have a glass. _____
5. She reads in church. _____
6. The wife is happy. _____
7. I need a tomato. _____

H5. Make correct sentences.

1. a-Liz-my-friend-is-sister-of   *Liz is a friend of my sister.*
2. Spanish-not-she-practice-does _____
3. many-you-books-how-have-do? _____
4. clothes-hangs-here-she-the _____
5. need-more-they-do-dishes? _____
6. be-counselor-his-with-he? _____
7. keep-my-here-mom-spoons-the _____

H6. Change **Ann and Susan** for **Martha**.

Ann and Susan are friends of my sister Mary. **They are** 16 years old. **They speak** English. **They do not** practice Spanish in their homes.

Ann and Susan prefer to stay in my house. **They love** my kitchen and my bedroom.

Ann and Susan make my bed every day. **They arrange** the sheets, the bedspread, the pillows and the blanket. **They hang** the clothes in the closet. Also **they clean** the mirror, the bathtub and the shower in the bathroom. **Ann and Susan are** really good friends.

Martha is a friend of my sister Mary. _____

Chapter 4
Clothing

What to do in each section of every lesson...

A - Vocabulary Study

Section A includes the vocabulary that will be used throughout the lesson. Learning new vocabulary is basic to learning a new language.

Read the vocabulary several times.
If you are on Basic ESL Online:
Listen to the **English audio pronunciation**.
View the **native language translations** of the vocabulary.

Listen and read the vocabulary until you can understand the vocabulary without looking at the words.

B - Sentence Structure

Section B teaches students basic English sentences using the vocabulary in section A.

Read and **study** the sentences.
If you are on Basic ESL Online:
Listen to the **English audio pronunciation**.
View the **native language translations** of the sentences.
View the **grammar concepts** by clicking on the **information button** [i] .

Repeat the sentences as many times as needed. Continue to the next section once you can **understand** the sentences without looking at them.

C - Listening Exercises

Read the story or dialog several times.
If you are on Basic ESL Online, **listen** to the story or dialog while reading it several times.

Once you are familiar with the story or dialog, try to see if you can **understand** it by only listening without reading.

D - Conversation Exercises

Read the conversation dialogs several times.
If you are on Basic ESL Online, **listen** to the dialogs until you can understand them without looking at them.

Finally, try to **speak** the conversation dialogs by only looking at the pictures and key words.

E - Common Phrases

Many of the **common phrases** that are presented in this section are frequently used by the native English speakers in their everyday life.

Read the common phrases several times.
If you are on Basic ESL Online, **listen** to the common phrases while reading. **Listen** as many times as needed until you can understand the common phrases without looking at the sentences.

H - Written Exercises

The written exercises provide an opportunity to test what you learned in the lesson. You can never be sure of knowing something unless you can put it in writing.

You can check your answers by going to the **Answer Key Section** in the back of the workbook.

For information regarding **Basic ESL Online,** please visit **www.basicesl.com**.
🎧 Audio Pronunciaton of English & 📺 Native Language Translations.

Lesson #10

The Clothes

Index

Audio & Translations

English Audio available online for sections A-E.

Translations in various Languages available online for Sections A, B, and E.

www.BasicESL.com

1. T-shirt

2. blouse

3. shorts

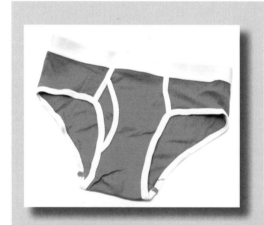

4. briefs

5. robe

6. pajamas

7. cap

8. hat

9. pants

10. skirt

11. shirt

12. tie

13. sandals

14. shoes

15. socks

16. suit

17. overcoat

18. dress

19. coat

20. jacket

21. sweater

22. jeans

Other Vocabulary

1.	n	kind	10.	v	share
2.	n	day	11.	v	belong
3.	adj	full	12.	v	smell
4.	adj	every	13.	v	fall
5.	adj	these	14.	v	suspect
6.	v	follow	15.	v	do
7.	v	sit	16.	adv	either
8.	v	wear	17.	adv	besides
9.	v	keep	18.	adv	then

B1. Verbs: Negative Questions

Tony **does not** wear a tie.
NQ **Does** Tony **not** wear a tie?

The boys **do not** wear suits.
NQ **Do** the boys **not** wear suits?

Erika **does not** wear dresses.
NQ **Does** Erika **not** wear dresses?

We **do not** wear jackets.
NQ **Do** we **not** wear jackets?

B1 - B2

*In English, **questions** in the negative form are not really questions denying something. They are used by the speaker when he is expecting or suspecting an affirmative answer. It could also be a suggestion or invitation. The answer to these questions can be affirmative or negative. With **verbs** other than the verb "**to be**", they are formed with "do" or "does".*

B2. Verbs: Negative Questions: Contractions

Fred **does not** wash his pants.
NQ **Doesn't** Fred wash his pants?

The boys **do not** make their beds.
NQ **Don't** the boys make their beds?

Mom **does not** arrange my closet.
NQ **Doesn't** mom arrange my closet?

Your socks **do not** smell bad.
NQ **Don't** your socks smell bad?

B3. Verbs: Present Tense: Short Answers

Don't you wear a gown?
Yes, I **do**.
No, **I don't.**

Doesn't she buy sandals?
Yes, she **does.**
No, she **doesn't.**

Don't I need shoes?
Yes, you **do.**
No, you **don't.**

B3

*In sentences with **verbs other than the verb "to be"**, a short answer is formed with the subject pronoun and the word "do" or "does".*

B4. Verbs: Short Answers

Do Susan and you share the clothes?
Yes, we **do.**
No, we **don't.**

Do they keep the sandals here?
Yes, they **do.**
No, they **don't.**

Does the house need drapes?
Yes, it **does.**
No, it **doesn't.**

B4

*In sentences with **verbs other than the verb "to be"**, a short answer is formed with the subject pronoun and the word "do" or "does".*

B5. Verb "to be": Short Answers

Is the gown beautiful?
Yes, it **is.**
No, it **isn't.**

Are the sandals big?
Yes, they **are.**
No, they **aren't.**

Are you the tailor?
Yes, **I am.**
No, **I'm not.**

B5 - B6

*In sentences with the verb **"to be"**, a short answer is formed with the subject pronoun and the verb **"to be"** only.*

B6. Verb "to be": Short Answers

Are the briefs expensive?
Yes, they **are.**
No, they **aren't.**

Is the handkerchief pretty?
Yes, it **is.**
No, it **isn't.**

Am I lucky?
Yes, you **are.**
No, you **aren't.**

C1. Read and Listen to the story.

My closet is full of clothes. I don't need many of these clothes. I have several shirts and pants, one suit with an extra coat, two jackets and an overcoat. I hang all these clothes in the closet.

I keep these clothes in the drawers of the dresser. I use the drawers for my socks, sweaters, ties, T-shirts, and belts.

My sister has a closet that is also full with clothes: skirts, blouses, a robe, all kinds of dresses and scarves. She wears different clothes every day.

C2. Read and Listen to the story of Anne and Susan.

Anne and Susan are friends of my sister Mary. They are 15 years old. They speak English. They do not practice Spanish in their homes.

Anne and Susan like to come to my house. They love my kitchen and my bedroom. The bedroom looks nice. It has beautiful drapes. The kitchen is big.

Anne and Susan make my bed every day. They arrange the sheets, the bedspread, the pillows and the blanket. They hang clothes in the closet. They also clean the mirror, bathtub and shower in the bathroom.

D1. Ann / skirt / shirt

Does Ann wear a skirt?
No, she doesn't wear a skirt.

Doesn't she wear a shirt?
No, she doesn't wear a shirt either.

What does she wear then?
She wears a blouse.

D2. boys / gloves / belts

Do the boys wear gloves?
No, they don't wear gloves.

Don't they wear belts?
No, they don't wear belts either.

What do they wear then?
They wear shoes.

D3. father / tie / cap

Does your father wear a tie?
No, he doesn't wear a tie.

Doesn't he wear a cap?
No, he doesn't wear a cap either.

What does he wear then?
He wears a hat.

D4. you / briefs / shorts

Do you wear briefs?
No, I don't wear briefs.

Don't you wear shorts?
No, I don't wear shorts either.

What do you wear then?
I wear pants.

Saying Hello

1. Hi Peter, how are you?
2. I am fine, and you?
3. I am fine too.
4. I can't complain.
5. How is your brother Mike?
6. He is great!
7. Glad to hear that.
8. Well, I have to go now.
9. Good to see you.
10. Say hello to Mike.

For the English audio pronunciations and written native language translations of **section E,** please go to:

www.basicesl.com

Well, I have to go now.

Good to see you.

End of the **oral exercises** for lesson 10.
You can find additional exercises in sections D, F & G at Basic ESL Online.

Please continue with the **written exercises** for this lesson in **section H.**

Lesson **10**

H1. Answer the questions with short answers.

1. Does **Carol** need sandals?

   *Yes, she **does**.*
   *No, she **doesn't**.*

2. Does Fred wear shorts?

   _____

3. Do they buy many clothes?

   _____

4. Does the school have a flag?

   _____

5. Does Lydia like the blouses?

   _____

6. Do you wear an overcoat?

   _____

7. Does the man want a hat?

   _____

8. Do you and Liz open the doors?

   _____

H2. Make negative questions.

1. Sharon **does not** follow the rules.

   ***Does** Sharon **not** follow the rules?*
   ***Doesn't** Sharon follow the rules?*

2. The boys **do not** wear suits to school.

   _____

   _____

3. My sister Jane **does not** hang her clothes.

   _____

   _____

4. The jackets **do not** belong to Edward.

   _____

   _____

5. Mary **does not** do homework at home.

   _____

   _____

6. The two brothers **do not** share their clothes.

   _____

   _____

7. The old clothes **do not** smell bad.

   _____

   _____

8. Denise **does not** like the new sweaters.

   _____

   _____

H3. Answer the questions with short answers.

1. Is the jacket short?   *Yes, it is.*
                            No, it isn't.

2. Are the belts strong?   _____

3. Are the jeans heavy?   _____
                            _____

4. Is the sweater too long? _____

5. Are the skirts too low? _____
                            _____

6. Are you happy with the hat? _____
                            _____

H4. Complete with the possessive adjectives.

1. You wear   *your own*   clothes.
2. I buy   _____   shoes.
3. Liz cleans   _____   dresses.
4. Frank washes   _____   pants
5. We wear   _____   suits.
6. You and I wear   _____   ties.
7. Ted and Greg wash   _____   socks.
8. Mary and Greg buy   _____   sweaters.
9. The school buys   _____   uniforms.
10. Sara and you clean _____   dresses.
11. Sara and I wear   _____   sandals.

H5. Follow the example.

1. Cynthia / robe

suit

Does Cynthia not wear a suit?
No, she does not wear a suit.

Doesn't she wear a robe either?
Yes, she wears a robe.

2. children / shoes

sandals

_____

_____

_____

_____

3. Henry / hat

cap

_____

_____

_____

_____

4. you / pants

shorts

_____

_____

_____

_____

5. women / blouse

shirts

_____

_____

_____

_____

Lesson #11

The Colors

Index

Audio & Translations

 English Audio available online for sections A-E.

 Translations in various Languages available online for Sections A, B, and E.

www.BasicESL.com

1. brown

2. blue

3. red

4. orange

5. pink

6. purple

7. gray

8. yellow

9. white

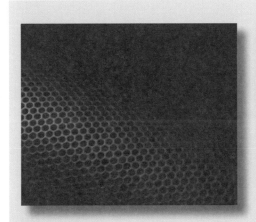
10. black

11. navy blue

12. beige

13. green

14. colorful

15. pink blouse

16. green shorts

17. gray hat

18. brown pants

19. blue shirt

20. white sandals

21. black overcoat

Other Vocabulary

1.	n	color	10.	v	forget
2.	n	uniform	11.	v	lose
3.	n	holiday	12.	v	pick up
4.	n	patron	13.	v	put on
5.	adj	gorgeous	14.	v	stop
6.	adj	filthy	15.	v	take
7.	v	sell	16.	v	take off
8.	v	choose	17.	adv	often
9.	v	undress	18.	pre	after

For the pronunciation and translation of **the sections A and B,** you can go online at:

www.basicesl.com

Looking for Bilingual Dictionaries?
You can find a large selection at:

www.bilingualdictionaries.com

B1. Substitution (S) of nouns with "one" or "ones"

	I have a blue **robe**.
S	You have a green **one**.
	You need a brown **overcoat**.
S	Henry needs a black **one**.
	We buy red **shirts**.
S	They buy yellow **ones**.
	I need beige **pants**.
S	Ray needs gray **ones**.

B1 - B2 - B3

Instead of repeating a singular or plural countable noun, they can be substituted by "one" or "ones".

B2. Substitution (S) of nouns with "one" or "ones"

	I want a white **car**.
S	I don't want an orange **one**.
	She sleeps in the soft **bed**.
S	She doesn't sleep in the hard **one**.
	She prefers pink **robes**.
S	She doesn't prefer green **ones**.
	The gray **shoes** are cheap.
S	The black **ones** are expensive.

B3. Substitution (S) of nouns with "one" or "ones"

	This is a different **skirt**.
S	It is not the same **one**.
	John is the strong **boy**.
S	Greg is the weak **one**.
	The new **books** are clean.
S	The old **ones** are dirty.
	My answer is the correct **answer**.
S	Your answer is the wrong **one**.

B4. Verb "to be": Short Answers

Is her blouse yellow?
Yes, **it is.**

Are her hats blue?
Yes, **they are.**

Am I a student?
Yes, **you are.**

Are you a teacher?
Yes, **I am.**

B4 - B5

Short answers with the verb *"to be"* consist of the **subject** and the form of the **verb "to be"** only.

B5. Verb "to be": Short Answers

Are all your dresses pink?
No, **they are not.**

Are you Mexican?
No, **I am not.**

Are all my socks white?
No, **they are not.**

Is your favorite suit green?
No, **it is not.**

B6. Review: Possessive Adjectives

I use **my** own pens.
You use **your** own pencils.

Mary writes **her** own books.
Tom buys **his** own notebooks.

We like **our** house.
My cousins like **their** house.

The girls like **their** bedroom.
The bedroom has **its** own TV.

B6 (Review)

C1. Read and Listen to the story of Henry.

Today is the holiday of St. Patrick. St. Patrick is the patron saint of Ireland. Henry wears green clothes to school. **He** likes to wear a green shirt, brown shoes, and red pants. **He** also wears a green scarf.

When Henry plays at school he changes his clothes. **He** takes off his jacket and puts on his T-shirt. This way **he** keeps **his** school clothes clean.

When Henry stops playing, **he** takes a shower. **He** often loses **his** clothes. **He** forgets to pick up **his** clothes after school.

C2. Read and Listen to the dialog.

What holiday is today?
It is the holiday of St. Patrick.

Who is St. Patrick?
He is the patron saint of Ireland.

What do the boys wear to school?
They usually wear green clothes.

What does Henry wear?
He wears a green shirt.

Does he wear green pants also?
No, he wears red pants.

What does Mary wear?
She wears a skirt and a blouse.

What color are they?
The skirt is white.

What color is the blouse?
The blouse is gray.

Does she wear a scarf?
Yes, she does.

What color is it?
It is yellow and brown.

D1. mom / yellow

What does your mom wear?
She wears shorts.

What color are the shorts?
They are green.

Does your mom prefer green shorts?
No, she prefers yellow ones.

D2. sisters / purple

What do your sisters wear?
They wear skirts.

What color are the skirts?
They are blue.

Do your sisters prefer blue skirts?
No, they prefer purple ones.

D3. you / pink

What do you wear?
I wear a dress.

What color is the dress?
It is brown.

Do you prefer brown dresses?
No, I prefer pink ones.

D4. uncle / blue

What does your uncle wear?
He wears a hat.

What color is the hat?
It is gray.

Does your uncle prefer gray hats?
No, he prefers blue ones.

Help with the language.

1. How do you say **pluma** in English?

2. You say **pen**.

3. I'm sorry, I don't understand.

4. Can you spell it, please?

5. It's spelled **P E N**. Is it clear?

6. Can you speak slowly?

7. One more time: *P E N*.

8. Is that clear now?

9. Yes, I get it now. Thank you.

For the English audio pronunciations and written native language translations of **section E,** please go to:

www.basicesl.com

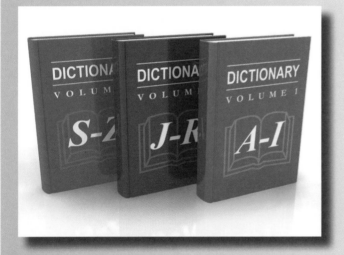

Can you spell it, please?

How do you say pluma in English?

End of the **oral exercises** for lesson 11.

You can find additional exercises in sections D, F & G at Basic ESL Online.

Please continue with the **written exercises** for this lesson in **section H.**

Lesson **11**

H1. Write the opposite adjective.

1.	black	*white*	
2.	cheap	_____	
3.	filthy	_____	
4.	first	_____	
5.	full	_____	
6.	funny	_____	
7.	gorgeous	_____	
8.	hard	_____	
9.	long	_____	
10.	new	_____	
11.	rich	_____	
12.	single	_____	
13.	strong	_____	
14.	ugly	_____	
15.	polite	_____	

big	_____
cold	_____
correct	_____
dirty	_____
easy	_____
happy	_____
light	_____
old	_____
previous	_____
same	_____
soft	_____
poor	_____
old	_____
young	_____
bad	_____

H2. Substitute the nouns with one or ones. Use the opposite adjectives.

1. You like **expensive shoes**.   *You don't like **cheap ones**.*
2. I use **small buttons**.   _____
3. He needs a **hard mattress**.   _____
4. We want the **same clothes**.   _____
5. The **young man** is tall.   _____
6. The **heavy blanket** is black.   _____
7. I prefer the **old socks**.   _____
8. They use the **hot water**.   _____
9. We like **big pockets**.   _____
10. They buy **white suits**.   _____

H3. Make correct sentences with the correct form of the verb.

1. sister-like-my-one-red-the   *My sister likes the red one.*
2. the-like-Diana-blouses-blue   _____
3. cuffs-with-pants-the-be-nice   _____
4. he-gray-does-wear-not-socks?   _____
5. many-ties-not-have-do-I   _____
6. practice-they-home-do-at?   _____

H4. Make the sentences plural.

1. Our family is big.   *Our families are big.*
2. The woman prefers a tray.   _____
3. I watch the child.   _____
4. He uses a sharp knife.   _____
5. The wife sits on the porch.   _____
6. She is in the library.   _____

H5. Follow the example.

1. coach / blue

   red jacket

   Does the coach like a red jacket?
   No, he doesn't.

   What does he prefer?
   He prefers a blue one.

2. you / black

   purple dress

3. Mary / yellow

   blue skirts

4. boys / orange

   pink ties

5. You-Liz / brown

   black shirts

H6. Change **Frank** for **my two sons**.

Frank wears green clothes to school because it is the feast of Saint Patrick, the patron of Ireland. **He** likes to wear a green shirt, brown shoes and red pants. Sometimes **he** also wears a green scarf.

When **Frank** plays at school, **he** changes **his** clothes. He takes off **his** jacket and puts on his T-shirt. This way **he** keeps all **his** school clothes clean.

When **Frank** stops playing, **he** takes a shower. **Frank** often loses his clothes. **He** forgets to pick up **his** clothes after school.

My two sons wear green clothes _____
_____
_____
_____
_____
_____
_____
_____
_____
_____
_____
_____
_____
_____
_____
_____
_____
_____
_____
_____
_____
_____

Lesson #12

Buying Clothes

Index

Audio & Translations

English Audio available online for sections A-E.

Translations in various Languages available online for Sections A, B, and E.

www.BasicESL.com

1. fabric

2. thread

3. iron

4. sew

5. wrinkles

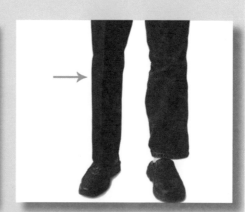
6. crease

7. pocket

8. label

9. zipper

10. sleeve

11. button

12. cuff

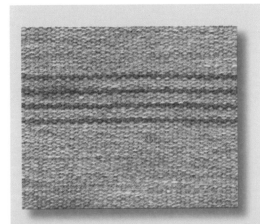

13. stripe

14. suspenders

15. handkerchief

16. gloves

17. scarf

18. belt

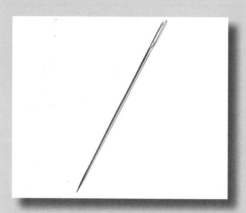

19. needle

20. knot

21. collar

Other Vocabulary

1.	n	choice	10.	v	lengthen
2.	n	corridor	11.	v	fade
3.	n	end	12.	v	fit
4.	adj	tight	13.	v	mend
5.	adj	famous	14.	v	try
6.	adj	elegant	15.	v	repair
7.	adj	loose	16.	v	shorten
8.	adj	torn	17.	v	shrink
9.	v	hold	18.	adv	okay

For the pronunciation
and translation of
the sections A and B,
you can go online at:

www.basicesl.com

Looking for Bilingual Dictionaries?
You can find a large selection at:

www.bilingualdictionaries.com

B1. Demonstrate Adjectives

		Near	Distant
S		**this** house	**that** house
P		**these** houses	**those** houses
S		**this** sweater	**that** sweater
P		**these** sweaters	**those** sweaters
S		**this** coat	**that** coat
P		**these** coats	**those** coats
S		**this** cup	**that** cup
P		**these** cups	**those** cups

B1 - B2 - B3

*Demonstrative adjectives are those that indicate the position of a person or thing in relation to the person who is speaking. If the person or object is close, we use "**this**" and "**these**". If it is distant, we use "**that**" and "**those**".*

B2. Demonstrate Adjectives

This sweater is expensive.
It is not cheap.

These fabrics shrink a lot.
They are not very good.

That belt is made of leather.
It lasts long.

Those shirts don't fit you.
They are too small.

B3. Demonstrate Adjectives

Those clothes are colorful.
They are very pretty.

Henry and I buy gray clothes.
We like that color.

That tie is nice.
It is very colorful.

I hate **these wrinkles**.
They are ugly.

B4. Information Question Words

Information Needed	Question Word Used
name	**What** is your name?
description	**What** is Mary **like**?
location	**Where** is she?
people	**Who** is that girl?
things	**What** does she study?
color	**What color** is the cap?
number	**How many** pens do you have?
choice	**Which** dress do you like?

B4

Questions words are those that we use to ask questions with the purpose of obtaining definite information. This information can be about the age, the name, the quantity, the description, the identification of people or things, the way we are or act, etc. They are especially important in conversations.

B5. Pronouns: Subject Pronouns (P)

The nieces are bad.
P **They** are bad.

The father is good.
P **He** is good.

The sister is beautiful.
P **She** is beautiful.

Joe is fat.
P **He** is fat.

B5 (Review)

B6. Pronouns: Subject Pronouns (P)

The lesson is short.
P **It** is short.

The lessons are long.
P **They** are long.

Helen and **I** are smart.
P **We** are smart.

Tom and **Mary** are young.
P **They** are young.

C1. Read and Listen to the dialog.

How can I help you?
I want to buy a dress.

Do you want a long dress?
No, I want a short one.

What fabric do you prefer?
I prefer a fabric that doesn't fade.

Does this fabric shrink?
Yes, it shrinks a little.

Do you want a solid color dress?
No, I prefer a colorful one.

Do you want to try this dress?
Yes, I do.

Where is the fitting room?
It is at the end of this corridor.

How does it fit you?
It is a little long.
We can shorten the dress.

How does it fit you at the waist?
It is a little tight.
We can loosen the dress a little.

C2. Read and Listen to the Story.

My closet is full of clothes. I don't need many of these clothes. I have several shirts and pants, one suit, two jackets and an overcoat. I hang all these clothes in the closet.

I keep these clothes in the drawers of the dresser. My dresser has nine drawers. I use the drawers for the following clothes: ties, belts, socks, T-shirts, briefs, and sweaters.

The closet of my sister is also full with clothes: skirts, blouses, a robe, all kinds of dresses.

D1. Karen / pink / blue

Is the skirt of Karen pink?
No, it isn't pink.

What color is it?
It is blue.

Doesn't Karen buy pink skirts?
No, she buys blue ones.

D2. Alex / green / red

Is the jacket of Alex green?
No, it isn't green.

What color is it?
It is red.

Doesn't Alex buy green jackets?
No, he buys red ones.

D3. Laura / black / white

Are the sandals of Laura black?
No, they aren't black.

What color are they?
They are white.

Doesn't Laura buy black sandals?
No, she buys white ones.

D4. uncle / brown / gray

Is the hat of your uncle brown?
No, it isn't brown.

What color is it?
It is gray.

Doesn't your uncle buy brown hats?
No, he buys grey ones.

Expressing wishes

1. I wish you were here.
2. I hope it rains.
3. I hope he gets well.
4. I hope he fails.
5. I hope he graduates.
6. I hope he gets a job.
7. I hope he succeeds.
8. I hope he recovers.
9. I wish you luck.
10. I wish you the best.

For the English audio pronunciations and written native language translations of **section E**, please go to:

www.basicesl.com

I wish you luck.

I hope it rains.

End of the **oral exercises** for lesson 12.
You can find additional exercises in sections D, F & G at Basic ESL Online.

Please continue with the **written exercises** for this lesson in **section H**.

Lesson

12

H1. Write the correct demonstrative adjective.

Near		Distant	
1. *this*	belt	*that*	belt
2. _____	gloves	_____	gloves
3. _____	hat	_____	hat
4. _____	pants	_____	pants
5. _____	pocket	_____	pocket
6. _____	scarf	_____	scarf
7. _____	shoes	_____	shoes
8. _____	sleeve	_____	sleeve
9. _____	suspenders	_____	suspenders
10. _____	sweater	_____	sweater
11. _____	zipper	_____	zipper
12. _____	wrinkles	_____	wrinkles
13. _____	thread	_____	thread
14. _____	button	_____	button

H2. Substitute the nouns with one or ones. Use the opposite demonstrative adjectives.

1. **This tie** is beautiful.   *That one is ugly.*

2. **These scarves** are short. _____

3. **These buttons** are small. _____

4. **Those pants** are tight. _____

5. **This belt** is too long. _____

6. **These coats** are expensive. _____

7. **This lesson** is difficult. _____

8. **Those women** are rich. _____

9. **That boy** is good. _____

10. **These dresses** are tight. _____

11. **This coat** is white. _____

H3. Ask the questions corresponding to these answers.

1. **That girl** is my sister.   *Who is your sister?*

2. Her name is **Mary**. _____

3. She is **elegant**. _____

4. She lives in **France**. _____

5. She learns **French**. _____

6. **Her dress** is yellow. _____

7. She wears **a cap**. _____

8. The cap is **red**. _____

9. She has **4** caps. _____

10. **She** needs only one cap. _____

11. The cap is **dirty**. _____

H4. Follow the example.

1.   Peter / green

red jacket

Isn't that jacket red?
   Yes, it is.

Doesn't Peter buy green jackets?
   No, he doesn't. He buys red ones.

2.   Laura / black

white sandals

_____
_____
_____
_____

3.   sister / pink

blue skirt

_____
_____
_____
_____

4.   school / gray

yellow gloves

_____
_____
_____
_____

5.   Liz / purple

pink blouse

_____
_____
_____
_____

H5. Select the correct answer.

1. A warm piece of clothing	sandals	T-shirt	sweater	shorts
2. An object with a knot	socks	tie	pants	jacket
3. An object used in pairs	coat	glove	hat	dress
4. An object used around the neck	sweater	pillow	thread	scarf
5. An object used as underwear	shoes	briefs	shirt	suit
6. An object used to cover the head	hat	suspenders	belt	robe

H6. Select the correct answer.

1. Does Alice _____ her clothes?   washes, cleans, wash

2. What are _____ ?   this, those, new

3. Does this shirt_____ ?   shrinks, blue, shrink

4. _____ Fred and you brothers?   Does, Are, Is

5. _____ black shoes are too big.   Do, A, The

6. Sara _____ buy dresses.   doesn't, don't, do not

7. _____ is that?   Mary, What, Those

8. My father _____ on the porch.   doesn't, isn't, do not

9. Is _____ gown pretty?   ugly, the, white

10. Does Tony_____ my sweater.   has, wear, needs

Chapter 5

Foods

What to do in each section of every lesson...

A - Vocabulary Study

Section A includes the vocabulary that will be used throughout the lesson. Learning new vocabulary is basic to learning a new language.

Read the vocabulary several times.
If you are on Basic ESL Online:
Listen to the **English audio pronunciation**.
View the **native language translations** of the vocabulary.

Listen and read the vocabulary until you can understand the vocabulary without looking at the words.

B - Sentence Structure

Section B teaches students basic English sentences using the vocabulary in section A.

Read and **study** the sentences.
If you are on Basic ESL Online:
Listen to the **English audio pronunciation**.
View the **native language translations** of the sentences.
View the **grammar concepts** by clicking on the **information button** .

Repeat the sentences as many times as needed. Continue to the next section once you can **understand** the sentences without looking at them.

C - Listening Exercises

Read the story or dialog several times.
If you are on Basic ESL Online, **listen** to the story or dialog while reading it several times.

Once you are familiar with the story or dialog, try to see if you can **understand** it by only listening without reading.

D - Conversation Exercises

Read the conversation dialogs several times.
If you are on Basic ESL Online, **listen** to the dialogs until you can understand them without looking at them.

Finally, try to **speak** the conversation dialogs by only looking at the pictures and key words.

E - Common Phrases

Many of the **common phrases** that are presented in this section are frequently used by the native English speakers in their everyday life.

Read the common phrases several times.
If you are on Basic ESL Online, **listen** to the common phrases while reading. **Listen** as many times as needed until you can understand the common phrases without looking at the sentences.

H - Written Exercises

The written exercises provide an opportunity to test what you learned in the lesson. You can never be sure of knowing something unless you can put it in writing.

You can check your answers by going to the **Answer Key Section** in the back of the workbook.

For information regarding **Basic ESL Online,** please visit **www.basicesl.com**.
Audio Pronunciaton of English & Native Language Translations.

Lesson #13

Fruits

Index

Audio & Translations

 English Audio available online for sections A-E.

 Translations in various Languages available online for Sections A, B, and E.

www.BasicESL.com

1. apricot

2. apple

3. cherries

4. banana

5. coconut

6. fig

7. grapes

8. grapefruit

9. melon

10. mango

11. orange

12. peach

13. pear

14. pineapple

15. plum

16. strawberry

17. watermelon

18. tangerine

19. date

20. prune

21. raisin

Other Vocabulary

1.	n	store	10.	adj	sweet
2.	adj	sour	11.	v	taste
3.	adj	stale	12.	v	follow
4.	adj	tasteless	13.	v	get
5.	adj	tasty	14.	v	grow
6.	adj	rotten	15.	v	ask
7.	adj	ripe	16.	v	remember
8.	adj	juicy	17.	v	choose
9.	adj	crazy	18.	v	eat

For the audio pronunciations and written translations of **Sections A and B,** please go to:

www.basicesl.com

Looking for Bilingual Dictionaries?
You can find a large selection at:

www.bilingualdictionaries.com

B1. Present Participle: Regular Formation

Verb	Participle
enjoy	enjoy**ing**
want	want**ing**
try	try**ing**
follow	follow**ing**
ask	ask**ing**
listen	listen**ing**
say	say**ing**
be	be**ing**

B1

The **past participle** of the verb is generally formed by adding "**-ing**" to the main verb.

B2. Present Participle: Irregular Formation

Verb	Participle
love	lov**ing**
have	hav**ing**
use	us**ing**
like	lik**ing**
fit	fit**ting**
sit	sit**ting**
begin	beginn**ing**

B2

Verbs ending in "**-e**" silent, drop the **e** before adding "**-ing**".

Verbs ending in a **stressed** single consonant, double the consonant before adding "**-ing**".

B3. Present Progressive Form: Present Tense

	I	**am**	**working**	late.
	You	**are**	**working**	late.
Singular	He	**is**	**working**	late.
	She	**is**	**working**	late.
	It	**is**	**working**	fine.
	We	**are**	**working**	early.
Plural	You	**are**	**working**	early.
	They	**are**	**working**	early.

B3

The **progressive** or **continuous form** of the verb is used to describe an action not completed and that still continues at the moment of speaking.

It is formed with the verb "**to be**" in the present tense and the **present participle** of the main verb ending in "**-ing**".

B4. Verbs: Progressive Form (PF)

Every day **I eat** grapes.
PF   Today **I am eating** figs.

Every day **you eat** bananas.
PF   Today **you are eating** watermelon.

Every day **he eats** strawberries.
PF   Today **he is eating** peaches.

Sue always **arrives** late.
PF   Today **she is arriving** early.

B5. Verbs: Progressive Form (PF)

Every day **she eats** oranges.
PF   Today **she is eating** tangerines.

Every day **we eat** pears.
PF   Today **we are eating** plums.

Every day **they eat** bananas.
PF   Today **they are eating** cherries.

We always **ask** for cherries.
PF   Today **we are asking** for grapes.

B4 - B5

*The **progressive** or **continuous form** of the verb is used to describe an action not completed, and that still continues at the moment of speaking. It is formed with the verb **"to be"** in the present tense, and the **present participle** of the main verb ending in "–ing".*

B6. Math Operations

multiplication $3 \times 3 = 9$
Three **multiplied by** three equals nine.

subtraction $11 - 11 = 0$
Eleven **minus** eleven equals zero.

addition $4 + 2 = 6$
Four **plus** two equals six.

division $20 / 4 = 5$
Twenty **divided by** 4 equals five.

B6 (Review)

C1. Read and Listen to the story.

Every day I go to the store with my mother and my sisters. My father **stays** at home working in his office or in the backyard.

Every day my mom **spends** 15 dollars for fruit. She **buys** different kinds of fruits. Her favorite ones are oranges, grapes and purple cherries. My little sister **chooses** peaches and apricots. My big sisters **ask** for strawberries or bananas.

Every day my parents **enjoy** pears and plums for dessert. I prefer to **eat** figs and tangerines.

C2. Read and Listen to the dialog.

Who likes fruit in your family?
My mom is crazy about fruit.

What fruit does your mom like?
She likes oranges and pears.

What color are the oranges?
They are orange.

What kind of fruit do you eat?
I eat plums, figs and bananas.

Are the figs ripe?
Yes, they are generally ripe.

What color are the plums?
They come in different colors.

Which ones do you prefer?
I prefer the purple ones.

What fruit does your sister buy?
She buys grapes.

Why does she buy grapes?
Because they are sweet and juicy.

Why doesn't she buy apricots?
Because sometimes they are stale.

D1. uncle / eat / orange

What fruit does your uncle eat?
He usually eats an apple.

Today he is eating an orange.
He is tired of eating apples.

Does your aunt eat an orange too?
No, she prefers the apple.

D2. dad / eat / cherries

What fruit does your dad eat?
He usually eats figs.

Today he is eating cherries.
He is tired of eating figs.

Does your mom eat cherries too?
No, she prefers the figs.

D3. boys / eat / melon

What fruit do the boys eat?
They usually eat bananas.

Today they are eating melon.
They are tired of eating bananas.

Do the girls eat melon too?
No, they prefer the bananas.

D4. father / eat / plums

What fruit does your father eat?
He usually eats grapes.

Today he is eating plums.
He is tired of eating grapes.

Does your mother eat plums too?
No, she prefers the grapes.

Asking a favor

1. Can I ask you a favor?
2. Yes, of course.
3. Can I borrow your pen?
4. Can I open the window?
5. Will you turn on the light?
6. Will you turn off the light?
7. Can you give me a ride to school?
8. Will you lend me a dollar?
9. Can you help me with this box?

For the English audio pronunciations and written native language translations of **section E,** please go to:

www.basicesl.com

Can you give me a ride to school?

Will you lend me a dollar?

End of the **oral exercises** for lesson 13.

You can find additional exercises in sections D, F & G at Basic ESL Online.

Please continue with the **written exercises** for this lesson in **section H.**

Lesson **13**

H1. Write the present participle of these verbs.

1.	add	*adding*	try	_____
2.	arrange	_____	ask	_____
3.	be	_____	close	_____
4.	begin	_____	fit	_____
5.	buy	_____	follow	_____
6.	choose	_____	have	_____
7.	cover	_____	put	_____
8.	divide	_____	stay	_____
9.	drink	_____	take	_____
10.	talk	_____	set	_____
11.	end	_____	watch	_____
12.	multiply	_____	do	_____
13.	fade	_____	use	_____
14.	sell	_____	sit	_____
15.	get	_____	taste	_____

H2. Change to the progressive form.

1. I **eat** grapes.   *I am eating* grapes.
2. You **eat** a melon.   _____
3. He **eats** apples.   _____
4. She **eats** bananas.   _____
5. It **works** fine.   _____
6. We **eat** oranges.   _____
7. They **eat** cherries.   _____
8. Ray **eats** apricots.   _____
9. Jane **eats** figs.   _____
10. Mom and dad **eat** peaches.   _____
11. I **buy** strawberries.   _____

H3. Change *every day* for *today*, using the words in (...).

Every day...   **Today...**

1. she **cleans** the dishes. (cups)   *she **is cleaning** the cups.*
2. I **buy** apples. (pears)   _____
3. Mary **comes** late. (early)   _____
4. mom **irons** the pants. (sheets)   _____
5. she **wears** a blouse. (dress)   _____
6. we **drink** juice. (water)   _____
7. they **get** good grades. (bad)   _____
8. she **chooses** figs. (plums)   _____
9. I **sit** on the chair. (floor)   _____
10. he **plays** at home. (school)   _____
11. Tom **wears** shorts. (pants)   _____

H4. Ask the questions corresponding to these answers.

1. **Fred** is buying some pears.
2. Your niece is **8 years old**.
3. **Cherries** are expensive.
4. The fruit store is **big**.
5. Her dresses are **pink**.
6. She has **twenty** dresses.
7. You like the **black suit**.
8. The wallet is **in your pocket**.
9. This dish tastes **very good**.
10. He doesn't like **vegetables**.

Who *is buying some pears?*

_____

_____

_____

_____

_____

_____

_____

_____

_____

H5. Complete the sentence with the correct preposition.

1. The pencils are   *in*   the drawer.
2. The book is   _____   the desk.
3. Mike is playing   _____   school.
4. Diane is also   _____   the school.
5. Your mom is   _____   the kitchen.
6. My dad is working   _____   the roof.
7. Is your brother   _____   home?
8. Are your friends   _____   the house?
9. Do you practice Spanish   _____   Susan?
10. Do they write letters   _____   Spanish?
11. Do you like this pair   _____   pants?
12. My mom spends $10.00   _____   fruits and vegetables.
13. The bottle   _____   juice is empty.
14. The brown shoes belong   _____   Andy.

H6. **Change** everyday **for** today.

Every day I **go** to the store with my mother and my sisters. My father **stays** at home working in his office or in the backyard.

Every day my mom **spends** 15 dollars for fruit. She **buys** different kinds of fruits. Her favorite ones are oranges, grapes and especially big purple cherries. My little sister **chooses** peaches and apricots. My big sisters **ask** for pears or strawberries.

Every day my parents **enjoy** plums and figs for dessert. I **enjoy** bananas or tangerines.

Today I am going to the _____

_____

_____

_____

_____

_____

_____

_____

_____

_____

_____

_____

_____

_____

_____

_____

_____

_____

_____

_____

Lesson #14

Vegetables

Index

Audio & Translations

 English Audio available online for sections A-E.

 Translations in various Languages available online for Sections A, B, and E.

www.BasicESL.com

1. carrot

2. cabbage

3. cauliflower

4. cucumber

5. green beens

6. garlic

7. mushrooms

8. lettuce

9. onion

10. peas

11. potato

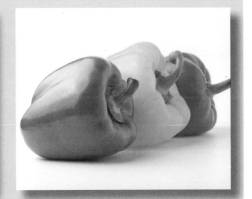

12. pepper

13. pumpkin

14. radish

15. sweet potato

16. tomato

17. vegetable

18. corn

19. asparagus

20. artichoke

21. spinach

Other Vocabulary

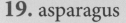

1.	n	dollar	10.	v	continue
2.	adj	popular	11.	v	go
3.	adj	annoying	12.	v	laugh
4.	adj	any	13.	v	offer
5.	adj	awful	14.	v	pay
6.	adj	famous	15.	v	refuse
7.	adj	free	16.	v	cook
8.	adj	quick	17.	v	spend
9.	adj	rapid	18.	adv	usually

For the audio pronunciations and written translations of
Sections A and B,
please go to:

www.basicesl.com

Looking for Bilingual Dictionaries?
You can find a large selection at:

www.bilingualdictionaries.com

B1. Progressive Form: Negative Sentences

I usually **eat** potatoes.
PF   Today I **am not eating** potatoes.

You usually **eat** onions.
PF   Today you **are not eating** onions.

Ann usually **eats** carrots.
PF   Today she **is not eating** carrots

We usually **eat** lettuce.
PF   Today we **are not eating** lettuce.

B2. Progressive Form: Negative Sentences

Henry always **asks** for corn.
PF   Today he **is not asking** for corn.

The store always **offers** free garlic.
PF   Today it **is not offering** garlic.

My mom always **cooks** mushrooms.
PF   Today she **is not cooking** mushrooms.

The uncles always **buy** tomatoes.
PF   Today they **are not buying** tomatoes.

B1 - B2

*Negative sentences in the progressive form of the verb are formed by placing the word **not** behind the verb "to be".*

B3. Indefinite Adjective: some, any

Aff   You have **some** rice.

Neg   You do not have **any** rice.

Q   Do you have **some (any)** rice?

Aff   We want **some** vegetables.

Neg   We do not want **any** vegetables.

Q   Do we want **(some) any** vegetables?

B3

Some and Any are indefinite adjectives that indicate a quantity not specified. Some is used in affirmative statements and questions. Any is used in negative statements and questions.

B4. Indefinite Adjective: some, any

Aff	She has **some** peppers.
Neg	She does not have **any** peppers.
Q	Does she have **some** (**any**) peppers?
Aff	I need **some** apples.
Neg	I do not need **any** apples.
Q	Do I need **some** (**any**) apples?

B4 - B5

Some and *Any* are indefinite adjectives that indicate a quantity not specified. *Some* is used in affirmative statements and questions. *Any* is used in negative statements and questions.

B5. Some, Any: Questions and Answers

	Do you write **any** letters?
A	Yes, I write **some** letters.
	Do you care for **any** fruit?
A	No, I don't care for **any** fruit.
	Does Martha spend **any** money?
A	Yes, she spends **some** money.
	Do they cook **any** vegetables?
A	No, they don't cook **any** vegetables.

B6. Some, Any: Questions and Short Answers

Do you have **some** onions?
Yes, I have **some**.
No, I don't have **any**.

Does Cathy need any **cabbage**?
Yes, she needs **some**.
No, she doesn't need **any**.

Does Bob cook any **carrots**?
Yes, he cooks **some**.
No, he doesn't cook **any**.

B6

*Short answers with **some** and **any** are formed by repeating the same verb of the question followed by **some** or **any**.*

C1. Read and Listen to the story.

Today I am going to the store with my mother and sisters. My father **is staying** at home **working** in his office or in the backyard.

Today my mom **is spending** 15 dollars for vegetables. She **is buying** different kinds of vegetables. Her favorite ones are onions, mushrooms and cabbage. Every day my little sister **is choosing** carrots and peas. My big sisters **are asking** for potatoes and green beans.

Today my parents **are enjoying** peppers and cauliflower with their meal. **I am eating** a vegetable salad with cucumbers and corn.

C2. Read and Listen to the story.

My closet is full of clothes. I don't need many of these clothes. I have several shirts and pants, one suit, two jackets and an overcoat. I hang all these clothes in the closet.

I keep the small clothes in the drawers of the dresser. My dresser has nine drawers. I use the drawers for the following clothes: ties, belts, socks, T-shirts, briefs, and sweaters

The closet of my sister is also full with clothes: skirts, blouses, a robe and all kinds of dresses.

D1. Mary-Henry / peppers

Is Mary cooking peppers with Henry?
No, they are not cooking peppers.
They are cooking carrots.

Do they have any carrots?
Mary has some.
Henry doesn't have any.

D2. I-Alex / cabbage

Am I cooking cabbage with Alex?
No, you are not cooking cabbage.
You are cooking potatoes.

Do we have any potatoes?
You have some.
Alex doesn't have any.

D3. Lucy-Greg / green beans

Is Lucy cooking green beans with Greg?
No, they are not cooking green beans.
They are cooking cauliflower.

Do they have any cauliflowers?
Lucy has some.
Greg doesn't have any.

D4. Paul-Sara / yams

Is Paul cooking yams with Sara?
No, they are not cooking yams.
They are cooking onions.

Do they have some onions?
Paul has some.
Sara doesn't have any.

Information on day and time

1. **What time is it now?**
2.   **It is two o'clock.**
3. **What day is today?**
4.   **It is Tuesday.**
5. **What month is this?**
6.   **It is January.**
7. **What date is today?**
8.   **It is May 6.**
9. **What year is this?**
10.   **It is the year 2011.**

For the English audio pronunciations and written native language translations of **section E,** please go to:

www.basicesl.com

What year is this?

What day is today?

End of the **oral exercises** for lesson 14.

You can find additional exercises in sections D, F & G at Basic ESL Online.

Please continue with the **written exercises** for this lesson in **section H.**

Lesson

14

H1. Change to the progressive *negative* form.

1. Liz usually **grows** corn.   *Now she is **not growing*** corn.

2. I usually **eat** potatoes.   _____ potatoes.

3. You usually **set** the table.   _____ the table.

4. Ann usually **pays** cash.   _____ cash.

5. She usually **works** at home.   _____ at home.

6. Joe usually **refuses** to eat.   _____ to eat.

7. I usually **go** alone.   _____ alone.

8. We usually **cook** at home.   _____ at home.

9. They usually **choose** pears.   _____ pears.

10. Fred usually **asks** questions.   _____ questions.

11. I usually **get** good grades.   _____ good grades.

12. The dress usually **fits**.   _____

13. I usually **sit** there.   _____ there.

14. He usually **wears** shorts.   _____ shorts.

15. This color usually **fades**.   _____ color.

H2. Complete the sentence with some or any.

1. You have | *some* | _____ | potatoes.
   Don't you have | *some* | *any* | tomatoes too?
   No, I don't have | _____ | *any* | tomatoes.

2. You don't need | _____ | _____ | mushrooms.
   Don't you need | _____ | _____ | cucumbers?
   No, I don't need | _____ | _____ | cucumbers.

3. Are you looking for | _____ | _____ | peaches?
   No, I'm not looking for | _____ | _____ | peaches.
   I'm looking for | _____ | _____ | pears.

4. Don't they care for | _____ | _____ | plums?
   No, they don't care | _____ | _____ | plums.
   They care for | _____ | _____ | chocolate.

5. Sorry, I don't like | _____ | _____ | pineapple.
   Do you like | _____ | _____ | bananas instead?
   Yes, I like | _____ | _____ | bananas.

6. I don't buy | _____ | _____ | lettuce.
   Do you buy | _____ | _____ | garlic?
   Yes, I buy | _____ | _____ | garlic.

H3. Answer the questions with some or any.

1. Do you have **some** onions?   *Yes, I have **some** onions.*

2. Does she have **any** corn?   *No, she doesn't have **any** corn.*

3. Do I need **some** rice?   No, _____

4. Do we need **any** vegetables?   Yes, _____

5. Does John want **any** fruit?   Yes, _____

6. Does Sara ask **any** questions?   No, _____

7. Do you prefer **any** carrots?   Yes, _____

8. Does she grow **any** peas?   Yes, _____

9. Do you eat **any** mushrooms?   Yes, _____

10. Do you care for **any** drink?   No, _____

11. Do you follow **any** rules?   Yes, _____

H4. Complete the sentence with the correct preposition.

1. The pencils are   *in*   the drawer.

2. The book is   _____   desk.

3. Mike is playing   _____   school.

4. Diane is also   _____   the school.

5. Your mom is   _____   the kitchen.

6. My dad is working   _____   the roof.

7. Is your brother   _____   home?

8. Are your friends   _____   the house?

9. Do you practice Spanish   _____   Susan?

10. Do they write letters   _____   Spanish?

11. Do you like this pair   _____   pants?

H5. Follow the example.

1. Henry   Mary

carrot

Do Henry and Mary **have** any carrots?
>   Henry has some.
>   Mary doesn't have any.

2. you   Lisa

potato

Do you and Lisa **need** any potatoes?

_____

_____

3. Ann   Paul

corn

Do Ann and Paul **buy** any corn?

_____

_____

4. boys   girls

garlic

Do the boys and girls **eat** some garlic?

_____

_____

5. Alex   Peter

onion

Do Alex and Peter **want** any onions?

_____

_____

Lesson #15

At the Supermarket

Index

Audio & Translations

 English Audio available online for sections A-E.

 Translations in various Languages available online for Sections A, B, and E.

www.BasicESL.com

1. dust pan

2. aluminum foil

3. bottle of juice

4. carton of milk

5. can of tomatoes

6. groceries

7. box of cookies

8. six pack of soda

9. jar of coffee

10. loaf of bread

11. utensils

12. paper towel

13. dozen eggs

14. bar of soap

15. nuts

16. bag of candy

17. pastry

18. olives

19. lentils

20. ketchup

21. mustard

Other Vocabulary

1.	n	aisle	10.	v	drink
2.	n	cart	11.	v	hate
3.	n	entrance	12.	v	shop
4.	adj	cheap	13.	v	purchase
5.	adj	expensive	14.	v	end
6.	adj	frozen	15.	v	finish
7.	adj	lazy	16.	v	warn
8.	v	look for	17.	adv	never
9.	v	find	18.	adv	why

For the pronunciation and translation of **the sections A and B,** you can go online at:

www.basicesl.com

B1. Verbs: Progressive Form: **Questions (Q)**

You **are looking** for rice.

Q **Are** you **looking** for rice?

He **is finishing** the work.

Q **Is** he **finishing** the work?

She **is drinking** milk.

Q **Is** she **drinking** milk?

We **are eating** cabbage.

Q **Are** we **eating** cabbage?

B2. Verbs: Progressive Form: **Questions (Q)**

Mark is **buying** coffee.

Q **Is** Mark **buying** coffee?

My parents are **paying** cash.

Q **Are** my parents **paying** cash?

Tom **is laughing** at me.

Q **Is** Tom **laughing** at me?

The boys **are smiling** at the girls.

Q **Are** the boys **smiling** at the girls?

B3. Verbs: Progressive Form: **Questions (Q)**

Mark **is not buying** coffee.

Q **Is** Mark **not buying** coffee?

My parents **are not working**.

Q **Are** my parents **not working**?

Tom is **not laughing** at me.

Q **Is** Tom **not laughing** at me?

The boys **are not smiling**.

Q **Are** the boys **not smiling**?

B1 - B2 - B3

Questions in the progressive or continuous form are formed by placing the verb "to be" in front of the subject of the sentence.

B4. Progressive form: **Substitution of nouns**

B4 (Review)

I want a white **car.**
I don't want an orange **one.**

She sleeps on the soft **bed.**
She doesn't sleep in the hard **one.**

She prefers pink **robes.**
She doesn't prefer green **ones.**

The gray **shoes** are cheap.
The black **ones** are expensive.

B5. Demonstrative Adjectives

B5 (Review)

This sweater is expensive.
It is not cheap.

These fabrics shrink a lot.
They are not very good.

That belt is made of leather.
It lasts long.

Those shirts don't fit you.
They are too small.

B6. Demonstrative Adjectives

B6 (Review)

Those clothes are colorful.
They are very pretty.

Henry and I buy gray clothes.
We like that color.

That tie is nice.
It is very colorful.

I hate **these wrinkles.**
They are ugly.

C1. Read and Listen to the story.

Today I **am going** to the supermarket with my mother and my sisters. My father **is staying** at home. My mom **is taking** a shopping cart from the entrance of the store.

Mom **is buying** several things for the kitchen and the pantry. She **needs** a carton of milk, a jar of coffee, three bottles of juice and a loaf of bread. I **am looking** for cans of tomatoes, a box of cookies, some napkins and utensils.

Mom **is paying** cash for the groceries. She **is not using** credit cards. Afterwards, she puts the groceries inside the paper bags. She takes the bags to the car and returns home.

C2. Read and Listen to the dialog.

Where is your mom going today?
She is going to the supermarket.

Who is going with your mom?
My sisters are.

Are you going too?
Yes, I am.

Is your father going with your mom?
No, he is staying at home

Is your mom using a shopping cart?
Yes, she is.

How is she paying for the groceries?
She is paying cash.

Where does she pay?
She pays at the cashier counter.

Where is the cashier?
At the exit of the store.

Where are the shopping carts?
They are at the entrance.

What is your mom buying?
She is buying a few things.

D1. Ann / to buy

Does Ann buy any tomatoes?
Yes, she buys cans of tomatoes.

Is she buying any tomatoes today?
No, she isn't buying any today.

Why is she not buying tomatoes?
Because she's tired of tomatoes.

D2. uncles / to ask

Do your uncles ask for any coffee?
Yes, they ask for jars of coffee.

Are they asking for any coffee today?
No, they aren't asking for any today.

Why are they not asking for coffee?
Because they are tired of coffee.

D3. boy / to buy

Does the boy buy any candy?
Yes, he buys bags of candy.

Is he buying any candy today?
No, he isn't buying any today.

Why is he not buying candy?
Because he's tired of candy.

D4. wife / to sell

Does the wife sell any bread?
Yes, she sells loaves of bread.

Is she selling any bread today?
No, she isn't selling any today.

Why is she not selling bread?
Because she is tired of bread.

Asking a favor

1. At what time does the train arrive?

2.   It arrives at 9:00 am.

3. At what time does the train leave?

4.   It leaves at nine-fifteen.

5. What time does the class start?

6.   It starts in 10 minutes.

7. How long is the class?

8.   It is one hour long.

9. What time does the class end?

9.   It ends at ten o'clock.

For the English audio pronunciations and written native language translations of **section E,** please go to:

www.basicesl.com

At what time does the train leave?

It starts in 10 minutes.

End of the **oral exercises** for lesson 15.

You can find additional exercises in sections D, F & G at Basic ESL Online.

Please continue with the **written exercises** for this lesson in **section H**.

H1. Change to Questions.

1. Carol **is eating** plums.   *Is Carol **eating** plums?*

2. Carol is not eating figs. _____

3. Sue is shopping today. _____

4. She is finishing the work. _____

5. We are drinking juices. _____

6. We are not drinking water. _____

7. You are warning Mary. _____

8. Lisa is not warning Joe. _____

9. Mom is buying groceries. _____

10. She is not buying pastries. _____

11. He is purchasing utensils. _____

12. He is not purchasing nuts. _____

13. The children are sleeping. _____

14. The children are not playing. _____

H2. Ask questions in the progressive form.

1. **My father** doesn't work in the garage every day.

   *Is **he** not working in the garage today?*

2. My nephews don't wear shoes every day.

   _____

3. Rachel does not wash her clothes every day.

   _____

4. Your mom does not go to the store every day.

   _____

5. Tom does not clean the spoons and forks every day.

   _____

6. Your brothers don't come here every day.

   _____

7. The children don't do homework every day.

   _____

8. My family does not watch TV every day.

   _____

9. Charles and Margaret don't clean the house every day.

   _____

H3. Select the correct answer.

1. **a hard fruit**	orange	grape	apple	fig
2. **a big vegetable**	potato	radish	pumpkin	tomato
3. **a vegetable with leaves**	carrots	mushrooms	potatoes	lettuce
4. **a fruit not juicy**	watermelon	pineapple	banana	pear
5. **Which one is round and green?**	tomato	cucumber	corn	pea
6. **a sweet vegetable**	pepper	yam	onion	garlic

H4. Multiple choice exercise.

1. They are _____ tennis shoes.   wears, wear, **wearing**

2. Does Tony _____ vegetables?   eats, eat, eating

3. Is Jane _____ raisins?   eats, eat, eating

4. Are you _____ for a bar of soap?   looks, look, looking

5. _____ does your sister prefer?   What, Who, Does

6. I am looking for _____ candy.   some, any

7. I don't want _____ kitchen towels.   some, any

8. I eat _____ kinds of soup.   some, any

9. _____ toilet paper is white.   A, The, What

10. My sister _____ not wash dishes.   is, do, does

H5. **Change** Today **for** Every day.

Today I am going to the store with my mother and my sister Ann. My father **is staying** at home.

Mom **is taking** a shopping cart from the entrance of the store. Mom **is buying** some things for the pantry. She **is not buying** things for the kitchen. She is **looking** for a jar of coffee, three bottles of juice and a loaf of bread. Ann and I **are looking** for boxes of cookies. We **are not looking** for fruit or vegetables.

Mom **is not paying** cash for the groceries. She **is using** one of her credit cards. Afterwards she **is driving** home. She **is not walking** home with the groceries.

Every day I go to _____

_____

_____

_____

_____

_____

_____

_____

_____

_____

_____

_____

_____

_____

_____

_____

_____

_____

_____

_____

ANSWER KEY SECTION

BASIC ESL WORKBOOK LEVEL 1

Chapter 1

H1

1. the sisters
2. the aunts
3. the husbands
4. the nephews
5. the sentences
6. the nieces
7. the brothers
8. the lessons
9. the exercises
10. the mothers
11. the articles
12. the cousins
13. the fathers
14. the daughters
15. the relatives

H2

1. a
2. an
3. a
4. a
5. a
6. a
7. a
8. a
9. an
10. a
11. an
12. a
13. a
14. a
15. a

H3

1. is
2. are
3. is
4. am
5. is
6. are
7. is
8. are
9. is
10. is
11. is
12. is
13. am
14. is
15. are
16. are

H4

1. they
2. we
3. you
4. they
5. they

H1

1. poor
2. short
3. ugly
4. small
5. single
6. ugly
7. fat
8. handsome
9. young
10. big
11. sad
12. rich

H2

1. husband
2. uncle
3. nephew
4. father
5. brother
6. grandfather
7. son
8. brother-in-law
9. cousin
10. relative

H3

1. They
2. She
3. It
4. He
5. He
6. They
7. She
8. He
9. She
10. They
11. We
12. It
13. You
14. It
15. They
16. He (She)
17. It
18. They
19. He
20. You
21. We
22. He
23. It
24. They
25. She

H4

1. Mary is not poor.
2. You are not short.
3. She is not ugly.
4. I am not married.
5. He is not sad.
6. They are not fat.
7. We are not ugly.

H5

1. Pat and Steven are tall.
2. The nephew is small.
3. You are not his cousin.
4. What is Mary like?
5. I am tall and happy.
6. The brother is not ugly.
7. He is not my brother.

H6

1. is
2. is not
3. is
4. is not
5. are
6. are not

H7

1. What is Tom like?
   He is thin.
   He is not fat.

2. What is the grandfather like?
   He is old.
   He is not young.

3. What are Lisa and Carol like?
   They are married.
   They are not single.

4. What are you like?
   I am tall.
   I am not short.

5. What are the sisters like?
   They are beautiful.
   They are not ugly.

H1

1. love
2. love
3. loves
4. loves
5. love
6. love
7. loves
8. loves
9. love
10. loves
11. love
12. love
13. love
14. love
15. loves

H2

1. poor
2. big
3. short
4. small
5. married
6. beautiful
7. thin
8. ugly
9. son
10. mother
11. sister
12. wife
13. cousin
14. aunt
15. young

H3

1. listen
2. comes
3. live
4. love
5. starts
6. come
7. love
8. lives
9. live
10. listens
11. lives
12. loves
13. starts
14. comes
15. loves
16. live
17. lives
18. listens
19. repeat
20. memorizes
21. asks
22. loves
23. come

H4

1. his
2. their
3. your
4. his
5. her
6. his
7. their
8. their
9. her
10. his
11. their
12. his
13. her
14. your
15. our
16. their
17. their
18. my
19. their
20. our
21. her
22. your
23. your
24. their

H5

1. One
2. Two
3. Three
4. Four
5. Five
6. Six
7. Seven
8. Eight
9. Nine
10. Ten
11. Eleven
12. Twelve
13. Thirteen
14. Fourteen
15. Fifteen
16. Sixteen
17. Seventeen
18. Eighteen
19. Nineteen
20. Twenty
21. Twenty-one
22. Twenty-two
23. Twenty-three
24. Twenty-four

H6

Tom is my friend. **He** comes from France. **His** uncle lives in France. **Tom** loves **his** family and **his** family loves **Tom**.

Tom lives with **his** parents and two other sisters. The parents love **their son Tom**, and he loves **his** parents also, especially **his** mother.

Other relatives of **Tom** are: **his** cousin Alice, **his** niece Susan, and Ray **his** nephew.

H1

1. She's
2. I'm
3. They're
4. We're
5. Mary's
6. Henry's
7. You're
8. He's
9. It's
10. She's
11. I'm
12. You're
13. It's
14. They're

H2

1. **She is not...**
   She's not...
   She isn't...
2. **You are not...**
   You're not...
   You aren't...
3. **They are not...**
   They're not...
   They aren't...
4. **It is not...**
   It's not...
   It isn't...
5. **We are not...**
   We're not...
   We aren't...
6. **I am not...**
   I'm not...
7. **He is not...**
   He's not...
   He isn't...

H3

1. **Where is your sister?**
   She's in the gym.
   She isn't in the classroom.
2. **Where are the boys?**
   They're in the classroom.
   They aren't on the playground.
3. **Where is the janitor?**
   He's in the hall.
   He isn't in the office.
4. **Where are the students?**
   They're in the auditorium.
   They aren't in the cafeteria.
5. **Where is Fred?**
   He's on the patio
   He isn't in the restroom.

H4

1. tall
2. poor
3. happy
4. young
5. single
6. fat
7. sister
8. mother
9. niece
10. cousin
11. daughter
12. aunt

H5

Mary and **Susan are** students. **They're** tall and beautiful. **They're** 13 years old. **Their** nationality is French. **They** come from France. **They** love this country.

They're very happy in the school. **Their** teacher is Mrs. Gonzalez. **Mary** and **Susan** speak French and English. **They** sit in the same class. I study with my friends **Mary** and **Susan**.

H1

1. Do
2. Does
3. Does
4. Do
5. Does
6. Do
7. does

H2

1. I do not know
2. You do not know
3. He does not know
4. She does not know
5. They do not know
6. We do not know
7. They do not know

H3

1. does not write
   is not
2. do not draw
   are not
3. does not enjoy
   is not
4. does not understand
   is not
5. do not study
   are not
6. does not love
   is not

H4

1. Three plus three equals six.
2. Four times two equals eight.
3. Five minus zero equals five.
4. Six divided by two equals three.
5. Twelve minus one equals eleven.
6. Two times ten equals twenty.
7. Thirteen minus four equals nine.

H5

1.
How old is Kathy?
She is twelve years old.
Kathy likes social studies.
She does not like art.

2.
How old are the girls?
They are nine years old.
The girls practice physical Education.
They do not practice music.

3.
How old are the boys?
They are eleven years old.
The boys love science.
They don't love math.

4.
How old is Rachel?
She is ten years old.
Rachel writes in Spanish.
She doesn't write in English.

5.
How old are your nephews?
They are eight years old
My nephews play at school.
They do not play at home.

H6

Pat **is not** my friend. She **is not** 12 years old. She **does not enjoy** art and music. She also **does not learn** geography with her teacher Mrs. Brown. Pat **does not love** her teacher. She **is not** from England. She **is not** twenty-three years old.

Pat **is not** smart. Her writing **is not** good. She **does not speak** good English. She **does not learn** Spanish and French at school. Spelling **is not** her favorite subject.

She **does not have** good grades in history and math. Her friend Lucy **does not like** social studies and sports. Her coach Carol **is not** her favorite teacher.

H1

1. Do you love...?
2. Does he love...?
3. Does she love...?
4. Do we love...?
5. Do they love...?
6. Does Greg ask...?
7. Does Tom shout...?
8. Does she speak...?
9. Does the class begin...?
10. Do we understand...?
11. Does Tony know...?
12. Does Jane draw...?
13. Do they write...?
14. Do we use...?
15. Does Henry want...?
16. Do I have...?

H2

1. **Yes, I ask**
   No, I do not ask
2. **Yes, they shout**
   No, they do not shout
3. **Yes, she speaks**
   No, she does not speak
4. **Yes, it begins**
   No, it does not begin
5. **Yes, they understand**
   No, they do not understand
6. **Yes, he knows**
   No, he does not know
7. **Yes, I draw**
   No, I do not draw
8. **Yes, she writes**
   No, she does not write
9. **Yes, we use**
   No, we do not use

H3

1. pen
2. blackboard
3. ink
4. scissors
5. notebook
6. glue

H4

1. an
2. loves
3. take
4. do not
5. isn't
6. aren't
7. has
8. How
9. study
10. learns

H5

1.
What does Mike have?
He has a ruler.
He does not have a blackboard.

2.
What do the boys have?
They have envelopes.
They do not have tables.

3.
What does the teacher have?
He has a wastebasket.
He does not have a flag.

4.
What do the students have?
They have lamps.
They do not have notebooks.

5.
What do you have?
I have a crayon.
I do not have a book.

H1

1. Is Mary...?
2. Are the windows...?
3. Is the balcony...?
4. Are you...?
5. Are the desks...?
6. Is Henry...?
7. Are the girls...?
8. Is the house...?
9. Are the doors...?
10. Is the hall...?
11. Is the ceiling...?
12. Is the porch...?
13. Is the apartment...?
14. Is the attic...?

H2

1. Is the doorbell small?
   Do the boys ring the bell?
2. Does he scrub the floors?
   Are the floors dirty?
3. Is the stove too big?
   Do we need a new stove?
4. Are the doors heavy?
   Does Frank close the doors?
5. Are the stairs pretty?
   Do you love the stairs?
6. Is the boy on the roof?
   Does he like to be on the roof?
7. Is the sofa new?
   Does mom sit on the sofa?
8. Are the windows small?
   Does Henry open the windows?
9. Does Jane sleep on the bed?
   Is the bed big?

H3

1. The boys are tall.
2. The nephews are here.
3. We use notebooks.
4. They rest on the sofas.
5. The girls want pens.
6. You prefer lamps.
7. My friends sit here.
8. They read books.
9. They are upstairs.
10. We are downstairs.

H4

1. Where is Tom?
2. How old is he?
3. What is he like?
4. What is he?
5. How many pencils does he have?
6. Where is his sister?
7. Who it tall?
8. What is she like?
9. What is her name?
10. What does she speak?
11. How many cousins does she have?

H5

1.
Are Tom and Alex on the roof?
No, they are not on the roof.
Where are they?
They are in the basement.

3.
Are they in the hall?
No, they are not in the hall.
Where are they?
They are in the kitchen.

5.
Are you and Liz on the porch?
No, we are not on the porch.
Where are you?
We are in the hall.

2.
Is Cynthia on the balcony?
No, she is not on the balcony.
Where is she?
She is in the garage.

4.
Is Fred in the backyard?
No, he is not in the backyard.
Where is he?
He is in the attic.

H1

1. children	16. deer
2. dishes	17. garages
3. families	18. halves
4. feet	19. knives
5. men	20. lives
6. mice	21. mattresses
7. potatoes	22. porches
8. sheep	23. shelves
9. teeth	24. trays
10. women	25. watches
11. churches	26. babies
12. geese	27. fishes
13. diagnoses	28. alumni
14. brushes	29. glasses
15. tomatoes	

H2

1. **The boys like the cups.**
   The blenders are old.
2. **The ladies are teachers.**
   They work in the libraries.
3. **The doors are heavy.**
   They knock on the doors.
4. **We watch the children.**
   They sleep on the sofas.
5. **The men need glasses.**
   His glasses are broken.
6. **The shelves are dirty.**
   They are near the babies.
7. **My knives are not sharp.**
   We need new knives.
8. **Your brushes are long.**
   You like short brushes.
9. **The churches are pretty.**
   They like pretty churches.

H3

1. Mary learns music.
2. They speak Spanish.
3. He loves our kitchen.
4. Does Frank clean the dishes?
5. Tom has two sisters.
6. We are in the same classroom.
7. We do not speak Spanish.
8. Do the boys like the blender?
9. They do not like the blender.
10. Where are the new brushes?

H4

1. Two **times** three equals nine.
2. Seven **plus** five equals twelve.
3. Thirteen **minus** nine equals four.
4. Eighteen **divided** by 6 equals 3.
5. Twenty **minus** fourteen equals 6.

H5

1. The knife is sharp.
2. I have a big family.
3. The porch is beautiful.
4. You have a glass.
5. She (she) reads in the church.
6. The wife is with the baby.
7. My life is happy.
8. I want a tomato.

H6

1.
What does Jane need?
She needs knives sometimes.
How many does she need now?
She only needs one knife now.

2.
What does mom need?
She needs mattresses sometimes.
How many does she need now?
She only needs one mattress now.

3.
What do the women need?
They need toothbrushes sometimes.
How many do they need now?
The only need one toothbrush now.

4.
What does the Tony need?
He needs mice sometimes.
How many does he need now?
He only needs one mouse now.

5.
What does the kitchen need?
It needs shelves sometimes.
How many does it need now?
It only needs one shelf now.

H1

1. The shower is not
2. Ann does not clean
3. The sheets are not
4. We do not wash
5. The bathtub is not
6. Mom does not clean
7. The blankets are not
8. Sara does not fold
9. The mirrors are not
10. I do not need
11. The drapes are not
12. The pillows are not
13. You do not need
14. The faucets are not
15. We do not need

H4

1. The knives are sharp.
2. We have a big family.
3. The porches are beautiful.
4. You have glasses.
5. They read in the churches.
6. The wives are happy.
7. We need tomatoes.

H2

1. Is Mark **not** tall?
   Isn't Mark tall?
2. **Are** the drapes **not** clean?
   Aren't the drapes clean?
3. **Are** the pillows **not** ugly?
   Aren't the pillows ugly?
4. **Is** the toilet **not** dirty?
   Isn't the toilet dirty?
5. **Is** John **not** a bad boy?
   Isn't John a bad boy?
6. **Is** the shower *not* new?
   Isn't the shower new?
7. **Are** the closets **not** big?
   Aren't the closets big?
8. **Is** the razor **not** sharp?
   Isn't the razor sharp?
9. **Is** the bedspread **not** small?
   Isn't the bedspread small?

H5

1. Liz is a friend of my sister.
2. She does not practice Spanish.
3. How many books do you have?
4. She hangs the clothes here.
5. Do they need more dishes?
6. He is with his counselor.
7. My mom keeps the spoons here.

H3

1. pan — fork
2. plate — knife
3. glass — spoon
4. stove — kettle
5. microwave — cup
6. blender — toaster

H6

Martha is a friend of my sister Mary. **She is** 16 years old. **She speaks** English. **She does** not practice Spanish in her home.

Martha prefers to stay in my house. **She loves** my kitchen and my bedroom. **Martha makes** my bed every day. **She arranges** the sheets, the bedspread, the pillows and the blanket. **She hangs** the clothes in the closet. Also **she cleans the** mirror, the bathtub and the shower in the bathroom. **Martha is** really a good friend.

H1

1. Yes, she does.
   No, she doesn't
2. Yes, he does
   No, he doesn't.
3. Yes, they do.
   No, they don't.
4. Yes, it does.
   No, it doesn't.
5. Yes, she does.
   No, she doesn't.
6. Yes, I do.
   No, I don't.
7. Yes, he does.
   No, he doesn't.
8. Yes, we do.
   No, we don't.

H2

1. **Does** Sharon not follow the...?
   Doesn't Sharon follow the ...?
2. **Do** the boys not wear...?
   Don't the boys wear ...?
3. **Does** my sister Jane not hang...?
   Doesn't my sister Jane hang...?
4. **Do** the jackets not belong to ...?
   Don't the jackets belong to ...?
5. **Does** Mary not do homework ...?
   Doesn't Mary do homework ...?
6. **Do** the two brothers not share...?
   Don't the two brothers ...?
7. **Do** the old clothes not smell ...?
   Don't the old clothes smell ...?
8. **Does** Denise not like the ...?
   Doesn't Denise like the ...?

H3

1. Yes, it is.
   No, it isn't.
2. Yes, they are.
   No, they aren't.
3. Yes, they are.
   No, they aren't.
4. Yes, it is.
   No, it isn't.
5. Yes, they are.
   No, they aren't.
6. Yes, I am.
   No, I'm not.

H4

1. your own
2. my own
3. her own
4. his own
5. our own
6. our own
7. their own
8. their own
9. its own
10. your own
11. our own

H5

1.
Does Cynthia not wear a suit?
No, she doesn't wear a suit.
Doesn't she wear a robe either?
Yes, she wears a robe.

2.
Do the children not wear sandals?
No, they don't wear sandals.
Don't they wear shoes either?
Yes, they wear shoes.

3.
Does Henry not wear a cap?
No, he doesn't wear a cap.
Doesn't he wear a hat either?
Yes, he wears a hat.

4.
Do you not wear shorts?
No, I don't wear shorts.
Don't you wear pants either?
Yes, I wear pants.

5.
Do the women not wear shirts?
No, they don't wear shirts.
Don't they wear blouses either?
Yes, they wear blouses.

H1

1. white	small
2. expensive	hot
3. clean	wrong
4. last	clean
5. empty	difficult
6. serious	sad
7. ugly	heavy
8. soft	young
9. short	next
10. old	different
11. poor	hard
12. married	rich
13. weak	new, young
14. beautiful	old
15. rude	good

H2

1. You don't like cheap ones.
2. I don't use big ones.
3. He doesn't need a soft one.
4. We don't want different ones.
5. The old one is short.
6. The light one is white.
7. I don't prefer the new ones.
8. They don't use the cold one.
9. We don't like small ones.
10. They don't buy black ones.

H3

1. My sister likes the red one.
2. Diane likes the blue blouses.
3. The pants with cuffs are nice.
4. Does he not wear gray socks?
5. I do not have many ties.
6. Do they practice at home?

H4

1. Our families are big.
2. The women prefer trays.
3. We watch the children.
4. They use sharp knives.
5. The wives sit on the porches.
6. They are in the libraries.

H5

1.
Does the coach like a red jacket?
No, he doesn't.
What does he prefer?
He prefers a blue one.

2.
Do you like a purple dress?
No, I don't.
What do you prefer?
I prefer a black one.

3.
Does Mary like blue skirts?
No, she doesn't.
What does she prefer?
She prefers yellow ones.

4.
Do the boys like pink ties?
No, they don't.
What do they prefer?
They prefer orange ones.

5.
Do Liz and you like black shirts?
No, we don't.
What do you prefer?
We prefer brown ones.

H6

My two sons wear green clothes to school because it is the feast of Saint Patrick, the patron of Ireland. **They like** to wear green shirts, brown shoes and red pants. Sometimes **they** also **wear** green scarfs.

When **my two sons play** at school, **they change** their clothes. **They take** off **their** jacket and **put** on **their** T-shirts. This way **they** keep all **their** school clothes clean.

When **my two sons stop** playing, **they** take a shower. **My two sons** often **lose their** clothes. **They forget** to pick up **their** clothes after school.

H1

1.	this	that
2.	these	those
3.	this	that
4.	these	those
5.	this	that
6.	this	that
7.	these	those
8.	this	that
9.	these	those
10.	this	that
11.	this	that
12.	these	those
13.	this	that
14.	this	that

H2

1. That one is ugly.
2. Those ones are long.
3. Those ones are big.
4. Those ones are loose.
5. That one is too short.
6. Those ones are cheap.
7. That one is easy.
8. These ones are poor.
9. This one is bad.
10. Those ones are loose.
11. That one is black.

H3

1. Who is your sister?
2. What's her name?
3. How is she?
4. Where does she live?
5. What does she learn?
6. What is yellow?
7. What does she wear?
8. What color is the cap?
9. How many caps does she have?
10. Who needs only one cap?
11. How is the cap?

H5

1. sweater
2. tie
3. glove
4. scarf
5. briefs
6. hat

H4

1.

Isn't that jacket red?

Yes, it is.

Doesn't Peter buy green jackets?

No, he doesn't. He buys red ones.

3.

Isn't that skirt blue?

Yes, it is.

Doesn't your sister buy pink skirts?

No, she doesn't. She buys blue ones.

5.

Isn't that blouse pink?

Yes, it is.

Doesn't Lisa buy purple blouses?

No, she doesn't. She buys pink ones.

2.

Aren't those sandals white?

Yes, they are

Doesn't Laura buy black sandals?

No, she doesn't. She buys white ones.

4.

Aren't those gloves yellow?

Yes, they are.

Doesn't the school buy gray gloves?

No, it doesn't. It buys yellow ones.

H6

1. wash
2. those
3. shrink
4. Are
5. The
6. doesn't
7. What
8. isn't
9. the
10. wear

H1

1. adding	trying
2. arranging	asking
3. being	closing
4. beginning	fitting
5. buying	following
6. choosing	having
7. covering	putting
8. dividing	staying
9. drinking	taking
10. talking	setting
11. ending	watching
12. multiplying	doing
13. fading	using
14. selling	sitting
15. getting	tasting

H2

1. I am eating grapes.
2. You are eating a melon.
3. He is eating apples.
4. She is eating bananas.
5. It is working fine.
6. We are eating oranges.
7. They are eating cherries.
8. Ray is eating apricots.
9. Jane is eating figs.
10. Mom and dad are eating...
11. I am buying strawberries.

H3

1. ...she is cleaning the cups.
2. ...I am buying pears.
3. ...she is coming early.
4. ...she is ironing the sheets.
5. ...she is wearing a dress.
6. ...we are drinking water.
7. ...they are getting bad grades.
8. ...she is choosing plums.
9. ...I am sitting on the floor.
10. ...he is playing at school.
11. ...he is wearing pants.

H4

1. **Who** is buying some pears?
2. **How old** is your niece?
3. **What** is expensive?
4. **How** is the fruit store?
5. **What color** are her dresses?
6. **How many** dresses does she have?
7. **What** do you like?
8. **Where** is your wallet?
9. **How** does this dish taste?
10. **What** doesn't he like?

H5

1. in
2. in – on
3. at
4. in
5. in
6. on
7. at
8. in
9. with
10. in
11. of
12. for
13. of
14. to

H6

Today I **am going** to the store with my mother and my sisters. My father **is staying** at home working in his office or in the backyard.

Today my mom **is spending** 15 dollars for fruit. She **is buying** different kinds of fruits. Her favorite ones are oranges, grapes and especially big purple cherries. My little sister **is choosing** peaches and apricots. My big sisters **are asking** for pears or strawberries.

Today my parents **are enjoying** plums and figs for dessert. I **am enjoying** bananas or tangerines.

H1

1. Now she is not growing
2. Now I am not eating
3. Now you are not setting
4. Now she is not paying
5. Now she is not working
6. Now he is not refusing
7. Now I am not going
8. Now we are not cooking
9. Now they are not choosing
10. Now he is not asking
11. Now I am not getting
12. Now it is not fitting.
13. Now I am not sitting there.
14. Now he is not wearing
15. Now it is not fading.

H2

1.	some	
	some	any
		any
2.		any
	some	any
		any
3.	some	any
		any
	some	
4.	some	any
		any
	some	
5.		any
	some	any
	some	
6.		any
	some	any
	some	

H3

1. Yes, I have **some** onions.
2. No, I don't have **any** corn.
3. No, you don't need **any** rice.
4. Yes, we need **some** vegetables.
5. Yes, he wants **some** fruit.
6. No, she doesn't ask **any** …
7. Yes, I prefer **some** carrots.
8. Yes, she grows **some** peas.
9. Yes, I eat **some** mushrooms.
10. No I don't care for **any** drink.
11. Yes, I follow **some** rules.

H4

1. in
2. on, in
3. at
4. in
5. in
6. on
7. at
8. in
9. with
10. in
11. of

H5

1.

Do Henry and Mary have any carrots?
Henry has some.
Margaret doesn't have.

3.

Do Ann and Paul buy corn?
Ann buys some.
Paul doesn't buy any.

5.

Do Alex and Peter want onions?
Alex wants some.
Peter doesn't want any.

2.

Do you and Lisa need any potatoes?
I don't need any.
Lisa needs some.

4.

Do the boys and girls eat garlic?
The boys don't eat any.
The girls eat some.

H1

1. Is Carol eating plums?
2. Is Carol not eating figs?
3. Is Sue shopping today?
4. Is she finishing the work?
5. Are we drinking juices?
6. Are we not drinking water?
7. Are you warning Mary?
8. Is Lisa not warning Joe?
9. Is mom buying groceries?
10. Is she not buying pastries?
11. Is he purchasing utensils?
12. Is he not purchasing nuts?
13. Are the children sleeping?
14. Are the children not playing?

H2

1. Is he not working in the garage today?
2. Are they not wearing shoes today?
3. Is she not washing her clothes today?
4. Is she not going to the store today?
5. Is he not cleaning the spoons...?
6. Are they not coming here today...?
7. Are they not doing homework...?
8. Are they not watching TV today?
9. Are they not cleaning the house...?

H3

1. apple
2. pumpkin
3. lettuce
4. banana
5. pea
6. yam

H4

1. wearing
2. eat
3. eating
4. looking
5. What
6. some
7. any
8. any
9. The
10. does

H5

Every day I go to the store with my mother and my sister Ann. My father **stays** at home.

Mom **takes** a shopping cart from the entrance of the store. Mom **buys** some things for the pantry. She **does not buy** things for the kitchen. She **looks** for a jar of coffee, three bottles of juice and a loaf of bread. Ann and I **look** for boxes of cookies. We **don't look** for fruit or vegetables.

Mom **does not pay** cash for the groceries. She uses one of her credit cards. Afterwards she **drives** home. She **does not walk** home with the groceries.